The Journey

The Journey

A Dressage Training Compendium from
USDF Connection

Co-Published by
the United States Dressage Federation and
Half Halt Press, Inc.

The Journey:

A Dressage Training Compendium from USDF Connection

© 2008 United States Dressage Federation, Inc.

Book design and production: Sara Hoffman

Cover photos by Susan Stickle, www.susanjstickle.com

Cover Illustration by Jim Dobson

Co-Published by

United States Dressage
Federation, Inc.,
4051 Iron Works Parkway
Lexington, KY 40511
(859) 971-2277
www.usdf.org

Half Halt Press, Inc.
P.O. Box 67
Boonsboro, MD 21713
(301) 733-7119
www.halfhaltpress.com

Printed in China

Table of Contents

Table of Contents

Foreword

Each chapter in this book is an article that previously appeared in *USDF Connection*, focusing on a specific gait or movement at each level, from Training through Grand Prix. The lessons are "conducted" by USDF-certified instructors.

The United States Dressage Federation would like to thank Margaret Freeman, the wonderful judge and writer who worked with Maryal Barnett, Christine Rivlin Henke, Cindi Rose Wylie, Mary Flood, Courtney King-Dye, Heather Bender, and Kathy Connelly to produce this timeless series of insights.

We also thank the riders and their horses without whom this series would not have been possible.

Enjoy the journey.

Training Level Lesson

Working Trot

BY MARYAL BARNETT WITH MARGARET FREEMAN

BEFORE WE BEGIN

When I start working with a new student, first of all I check to make sure he or she knows about the training scale or "pyramid of training," if only the outline. Then we discuss how we will use the training scale to improve the gait or the movement in question through the use of gymnastic exercises. At Training Level, generally speaking, you will be working on the first three rungs of the scale: rhythm and regularity, suppleness, and contact (by teaching the horse to stretch to the contact, not by pulling back on the reins).

WORKING TROT: THE FOUNDATION

The journey through the levels starts with the working trot at Training Level.

The working trot is the basis for everything else that will be a part of the horse's education, from Training Level to the possible goal of Grand Prix.

It is the primary gait used in the training of a horse at this level because the trot is the most balanced gait

SUSANJSTICKLE.COM

GOOD ENERGY AND BEND in working trot, as displayed by Jacqueline Stapel on Atticus

and also because it has suspension (a moment during which all four limbs are off the ground). The combination of these factors makes the trot the best gait for gymnasticizing the horse in this early stage of his training. It is through the trot that the other gaits can be most improved. Because the quality of the walk is too easily destroyed if the horse is stiff through his back, working at that gait should be avoided unless it is ridden on a long rein, with the horse stretching his topline. Young horses usually are not yet balanced enough at the canter to use that gait for suppling. The canter can be used later for gymnastics, but not at this point in the training as a rule, for the young horse is still struggling to balance with the additional weight of the rider.

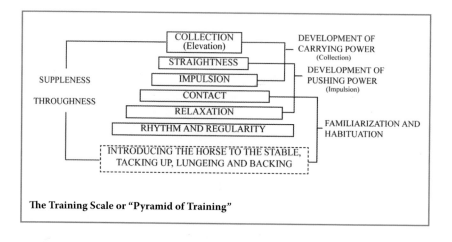

The Training Scale or "Pyramid of Training"

WARM-UP AND ASSESSMENT

If you were my student, I'd ask you to warm your horse up in a nice, forward, regular working trot rising, making 20-meter circles and changing directions so that your horse loosens his muscles on both sides. I'd watch your horse go, and then I'd let you know both the positive things that I observe and the qualities that need to be improved— perhaps a quick tempo, a stiff back, or a lack of suspension. Improvement of these flaws will help improve the quality of the gaits. To improve the working trot, we usually need to focus on the horse's suppleness and balance. If he is not on the bit, then we'd need to address that as well.

In the next phase of your lesson, you and I would discuss the qualities of the working trot that could use some improvement, and I'd explain how each relates to specific aspects of the training scale and how the use of simple gymnastic exercises and figures can help your horse develop better rhythm, suppleness, and stretch to the contact. Let's take a moment to look at each of these qualities in more detail as they relate to the working trot.

Rhythm and Regularity

In your dressage training, you are not only striving to improve the rhythm of the trot, but you're also using rhythm as a guideline to aid you in riding your horse in his optimum state of balance and gymnastic ability at that point in his training. For instance, if the trot rhythm becomes irregular, that's a red flag.

The quality of rhythm underpins the training scale because you'll use it as a benchmark all the way up through the levels. Here's an example. Later in your training, in a First Level leg-yield or a Second Level shoulder-in, you may find that your horse's trot steps become irregular at some point. You know that rhythm and regularity constitute the basis of the training scale, so you know that something is amiss in the fundamentals. Now your job is to determine what caused the irregularity: lack of suppleness, loss of balance, incorrect contact, or some other reason.

When you ride figures, pay attention that your horse follows the line with the bend throughout his whole body while maintaining a correct rhythm and steady tempo. That's a good goal. It doesn't have to be perfect every time, but you must always be aware of your horse's rhythm and tempo so that his schooling progresses in a positive manner, with as few setbacks as possible (although the occasional step backward is inevitable).

Suppleness

If the judges generally give your horse's basic working trot a score of 6, you can improve that mark by developing his suppleness, engagement, and balance through correct figures and transitions. Keep him as balanced over his hindquarters as his strength will allow so that he doesn't fall on the forehand. Although you'll strive to make your geometry and transitions as precise as possible, know that at Training Level the judges don't expect as much accuracy as they do further up the levels.

All of the levels of the training scale are interrelated, and suppleness is no exception. For example, there is a connection between suppleness and tempo (rate of repetition of the footfalls). Finding and keeping a horse's correct tempo is a real challenge for many riders, and many riders misunderstand the concept of tempo as well. The judge might say "needs more impulsion," and the rider responds, incorrectly, by making the horse go faster, in a quicker tempo. When a rider does that, she makes the horse's back stiff and therefore causes him to lose suppleness. The correct tempo, I believe, is one that challenges the horse to have energy but doesn't stiffen his back and cause him to go on the forehand.

Contact

It's so important that your horse learn to accept the contact without pulling. At the same time, you must allow him to stretch to the contact by allowing your elbow joints to open and close gently to accommodate the action of his head and neck. You set the parameters, but you always give your horse a little bit of space so that you feel as if you can ride his hind legs into that space. He then stretches toward the bit and reaches out of his withers.

Circles, serpentines, figure eights, and other exercises are not just movements in dressage tests. They're useful exercises that can be used in a variety of ways. The important thing about using exercises is that you give the horse variety by working both sides and not drilling him. To keep him interested in his work, you may want to do things like work over cavalletti (ground-level or slightly raised poles) and ride up and down hills. Using the exercises in a variety of ways so that the horse is challenged and interested makes for a more involved equine student. I'll help you to start a training program in which you ride the exercises in a logical order so that they build on one another.

EXERCISES FOR WORKING TROT

I'm going to give you three exercises for improving your horse's working trot. The exercises are presented in a logical order, from the most elementary to more advanced versions. Although I'm not discussing the canter in this article, realize that all of these exercises can and should be done at the canter as your horse's balance improves. Remember: keep the figures and movements varied, but don't drill your horse. Strive to keep him happy and interested in his work.

Exercise 1: 20-meter Circle

The first figure that I teach students is the 20-meter circle. Ridden correctly, this most basic of figures really gymnasticizes the horse.

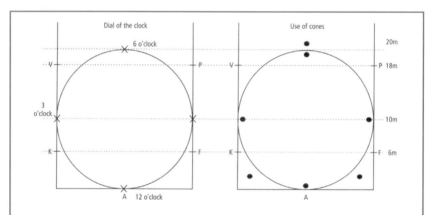

20-meter circles at A and C or B and E

- Equipment needed: Four cones, or draw lines in dirt
- Purpose: Rhythm, suppleness, accuracy
- Variables: Ride through each quadrant point. Complete both circles three to four times. Cross on diagonal. Repeat in opposite direction.
- Additional problems addressed: Necessity of correct figures; turning at each quadrant point; correct diagonal line when changing direction.

The most common error in riding the 20-meter circle is failing to make the figure truly round. I tell my students to imagine the hours on a clock face and to ride on the circle so that they touch the four points of three 0'- clock, six o'clock, nine o'clock, and twelve o'clock, while bending the horse so that his spine travels the circumference of the circle. As a visual aid, I set up four cones or markers inside the track indicating the four points. Instead of thinking of the figure as a circle, try going from point to point with bend. This concept will help you to remember to turn your horse with the outside rein instead of the inside rein—because using the inside rein to turn will cause your horse to "fall" on his outside shoulder.

Exercise 2: Three-loop Serpentine

The next figure that I usually teach is the serpentine of three equal loops because it is a further development of the 20-meter circle. In this figure, the horse changes the bend from one side to the other. This gymnastic exercise continues to develop his lateral suppleness as well as his rhythm and contact.

As in the 20-meter circle, the serpentine figure should be accurate so that your horse does not "cheat" by avoiding the difficulties that his stiff and hollow sides create. To help my students see the two places along the serpentine where they need to straighten the horse and then change the position and the bend, I again set up cones or markers to indicate how the 60-meter long arena divides into three sections of 20 meters each. After the rider is able to make a correct figure, I increase the difficulty by adding transitions to and from the walk or a halt crossing the center line.

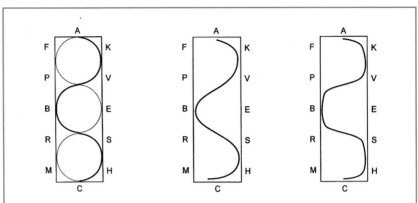

Three-loop serpentine

- Equipment needed: Cones, draw lines in dirt, or ground poles
- Purpose: Rhythm, suppleness, contact, accuracy
- Variables: Tie into 20-meter circle, which is the foundation; connect 20-meter circles one to another while changing direction.
- Additional problems addressed: Three equal loops; moment of straightness; changing bend; if energy is lost, ask for it on the long side

Exercise 3: Change of Direction through the 20-meter Circle

In this exercise, I insist that the change be performed on the center line. Doing so gives the rider a clear visual reference as to how to divide the 20-meter circle into two ten-meter half-circles. The change through the circle is a much more difficult exercise than most riders expect. Therefore, I very often have people walk their horses through the figure before asking them to try it at a trot.

I advise all my students to limit any exercise or movement to ten repetitions per schooling session, even if they're not 100-percent successful. Improvement comes with time. However, if that figure was the focus of the lesson, I might return to it later. The horse should be challenged but never bored or so physically

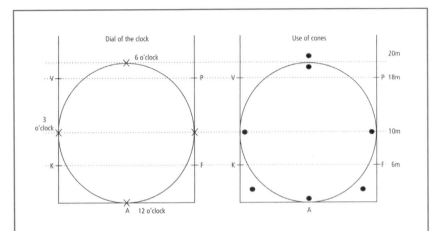

Change of direction through the circle

- Equipment needed: Cones, or draw two lines in sand on center line where two ten-meter half circles connect.
- Purpose: Suppleness; obedience to aids, especially outside rein.
- Variables: Tie into exercises 1 and 2, creating a more advanced exercise combining 20-meter circles plus serpentines. Start from walk.
- Additional problems addressed: Importance of using center line; equal ten-meter half-circles, maintaining the rhythm and tempo.

fatigued that he withdraws mentally or becomes injured from the repetitive stress. Horse and rider should develop a partnership so that the work becomes as much the horse's idea as it is the rider's. Neither people nor horses can learn when they are tired or defensive.

KNOW WHERE YOU'RE HEADED

Improving the working trot is the basis for all further development of the correct basics, which prevent injury and increase performance longevity. It takes years for a horse to develop muscle first, and then bone. It should be every rider's goal to progress and not to stagnate. Riders and trainers need to know where they're going. Dressage is not just riding circles and serpentines; it is about developing the horse to be a willing athlete. We are working toward training the horse to carry more from his hindquarters and, one day, if all goes well, to arrive at the Grand Prix level. The reward for proper training is that both the horse and rider will enjoy the journey.

First Level Lesson

Trot Lengthenings

BY CHRISTINE RIVLIN HENKE

BEFORE WE BEGIN

Before you start working on trot lengthenings, your horse must already meet the requirements of Training Level according to the training scale (see page 6). He needs a clear two-beat trot rhythm. He should show a comfortable level of mental and physical relaxation by accepting the rider and your aids, and by moving with a supple back. He should be able to maintain a consistent and energetic working-trot tempo.

I want my students to be aware that every horse develops at a different rate, and that there are times when the trot is stronger than the canter or the canter is stronger than the trot. As you work with your horse, keep in mind that each gait can help improve the others and that exercises done in one gait can, in the long run, help improve the other gaits.

NICE LENGTHENING: The writer aboard Nora McGee's seven-year-old Hanoverian mare, Larissa's Jas (by Lanthan), at First Level Test 4. I'd prefer it if her profile were slightly in front of the vertical.

LENGTHENING DEFINED

What we are trying to achieve with a trot lengthening is elongation of the horse's stride and outline. In a First Level trot lengthening, your goal is to demonstrate that your horse has developed an increased amount of balance, "throughness," and thrust (pushing power). With these objectives in mind, let's get our lesson started.

WARM-UP AND ASSESSMENT

If you were my student, I'd start by watching you warm up at the walk, trot, and canter in both directions to see where your horse's strengths and weaknesses lie at this point in his training. I like to check to see how my students feel about their horses' strengths and weaknesses so that we are on the same page. I like to keep communication open for student input as to what they are feeling, for what I see and what they feel is not always the same thing.

Before you even try to lengthen your horse's stride at the trot, you need to understand that, as you ask him to lengthen, you want to slightly increase your driving aids (seat and legs) to encourage him to take longer strides while remaining in an even tempo and in balance. When I ride, I want to influence my horse as his inside hind leg (that is, inside relative to the exercise) is leaving the ground. If you have access to mirrors, they can be helpful in sorting out which leg is on the ground and which is airborne. Here's a tip for learning to feel the motion of the hind legs: In posting trot, while your seat is still in the saddle but beginning to lighten at the start of the "up" moment, what

EXERCISE 2: Leg-yield to long side

ILLUSTRATION BY BETSY BELL

you feel under your seat is your horse's inside hind leg leaving the ground.

As you aim to produce a lengthening of your horse's trot stride, think of slightly increasing your seat aids to encourage him to "follow" your seat and take a longer stride. Your hands should remain in a soft, elastic contact with his mouth, neither pulling nor throwing away the contact.

One common rider error is to support or "carry" the horse with the driving aids at each stride. When I ride, I want to make sure that my forward driving aids produce an immediate reaction. However, a green horse might need a few more reminders to maintain the longer stride than a horse that is a bit further along in its training.

EXERCISES FOR TROT LENGTHENINGS

The following exercises are arranged from easiest to more difficult. There are many more variations. It's important to always keep the training scale in mind and to understand that, if you have major problems with an exercise, you might have to take a step back and find the "hole." Strive to find the exercises that work best for your horse at his particular stage of training to further develop him physically and mentally. Plan short- and long-term goals for your horse's training but know that we, as riders and trainers, have to be flexible with our equine partners. Finally, none of the exercises is meant to be drilled but more explored and "played with."

Do the exercises in posting trot first, especially if your horse is inexperienced and at a fairly elementary stage in his dressage training. Because your motion in the posting trot is more exaggerated than in the sitting trot, schooling trot lengthenings in posting trot at first will help you get the feel for the tempo and the timing of your aids. Plus, the earliest lengthenings in the dressage tests are ridden in posting trot.

Later, you'll work toward developing lengthenings in the sitting trot, and that's how you'll have to ride them in the dressage tests, beginning with First Level Test 3. The more difficult of the exercises I'll give you should be ridden in the sitting trot because you'll be able to influence your horse more with your seat. It's important, however, always to remain aware of how your horse feels. For example, if you begin riding a lengthening in the sitting trot but your horse's back starts to feel hollow, or if he isn't strong enough to sustain the lengthening in sitting trot, it's OK to go back to posting. It's fine to go back and forth at this stage of training. We are only talking about developing lengthenings, not medium trot or extensions, which require a greater degree of carrying power.

Exercise 1: 20-meter circle to long side

Establish a 20-meter circle in working trot at A or C. Exit the circle onto the long side of the arena, where your horse might naturally want to move more forward. As you start onto the long side, ask for a few lengthened strides—six to ten, or more if he is further along and able to maintain his balance. The approaching corner will be the natural place to return to the working trot because he'll see the fence or wall and "want to come back."

- **Possible problem #1:** Your horse loses balance and "runs," taking faster and more hurried strides instead of lengthening his stride while maintaining the tempo of the working trot.
  Solution: Go back onto a 20-meter circle to regain the working tempo and balance before trying the exercise again.

- **Possible problem #2:** He breaks into a canter.
  Solution: Return to the 20-meter circle without pulling back on the reins. Then calmly bring him back to a trot to reestablish rhythm, balance, and tempo.

- **Possible problem #3:** He won't come back from the lengthening and runs through your aids.
  Solution: Turn onto a circle without pulling back to politely insist that he must come back and follow your aids again.

Exercise 2: Leg-yield to long side

Establish a 20-meter circle at A or C in working trot. On the circle, position your horse in a leg-yield, with his hindquarters moving toward the outside of the circle. (Think of his forehand moving on a nineteen-meter circle and his hindquarters moving on approximately a 20-meter circle.) When he is positioned correctly, his inside hind leg will step well to the midline of his body while his back becomes loose, creating more swing.

From the leg-yield positioning on the circle, direct your horse onto a straight line down the long side of the arena. As you move onto the straight line, immediately ask him to lengthen his stride in the trot. A variation of this exercise is to come out of the leg-yield position but remain on the 20-meter circle and ask for the lengthening on the bending line of the circle. School this exercise in both directions so that you work both hind legs equally.

- **Possible problem #1:** Your horse finds this exercise more difficult in one direction.
  Solution: All horses at some point have a stronger and weaker side and hind leg. Although you'll always school an exercise to both sides, work the weaker or more difficult side in shorter periods of leg-yield.

Exercise 3: Lengthening on a bending line

Start at A or C and develop lengthened strides as you ride on a three-loop serpentine or a 20-meter circle. This is a great exercise to develop even push from both hind legs. It also helps the horse that anticipates lengthening across the diagonal and shortening before the corner. It teaches him to be more honestly on the aids instead of just going through a pattern that he's learned from the dressage tests.

Variation: Practice adjusting your horse's stride for short periods as you ride on the circle or serpentine: six strides forward, six strides working, and so on.

Exercise 4: Short diagonals to shoulder-fore

I refer to this as my "freeway and off-ramp exercise," where you rev up coming into the corner so you can hop onto the freeway (the diagonal) with sufficient energy. You wind down as you approach the off-ramp (the long side of the arena) using a slight shoulder-fore positioning to decelerate as you hit the off-ramp.

Ride working trot from H to B. As you come into the corner by H, ride a reasonably deep corner that sets your horse up for the short diagonal, getting his inside hind leg to come well underneath his body. As you ride onto the diagonal, ask for a quick response and a burst of energy into a trot lengthening.

As you approach B, position your horse into a bit of a shoulder-fore position, again to develop the ability of his hind leg to reach under in the transition back to working trot. He'll learn to follow your seat aids in the transition back to working trot, thus preventing you from pulling on the reins and causing him to stiffen.

- **Possible problem #1:** Your horse's hindquarters swing out in the first corner.
  Solution: Make sure before you start that you and the horse meet the training scale requirements, and that he readily accepts your aids and understands what you are asking. You might have to come back to the walk a few times and school him so that he doesn't push into your leg in the corner.

- **Possible problem #2:** He breaks into a canter as you turn onto the diagonal.
  Solution: Make sure that you are able to ride a balanced corner so that you can influence his hind leg to come under while he's still in the corner.

Exercise 5: Corner halts

Start on the right rein in working trot. Ride a fairly deep, balanced corner at M, revving and preparing your horse to come out of the corner in a lengthening. Then ride from M to F in lengthened trot. As you approach F, prepare to halt. A little shoulder-fore positioning may help the preparation. At F, halt. Ride a turn on the forehand from your left (outside) leg, and immediately move off at a trot, developing a second lengthening from F to M as quickly as possible. As you approach M, prepare to halt. At M, halt. Ride a turn on the forehand from your right (outside) leg, and move off immediately into another trot lengthening.

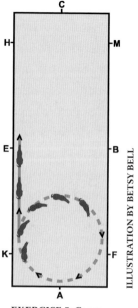

EXERCISE 5: Corner halts

- **Possible problem #1:** Your horse is reluctant to move forward promptly.
  Solution: With the corner to begin with, and then the halt and turn on the forehand all happening relatively quickly, he'll develop a sharper response to your aids.

- **Possible problem #2:** He resists the turn on the forehand.
  Solution: Go back to more basics through the training scale. Make sure that your horse is on your aids and that he fully understands the requirements of the more basic exercise of turn on the forehand.

Second Level Lesson

Three-loop Counter-Canter Serpentine

BY RACHEL SAAVEDRA WITH MARGARET FREEMAN

The Three-loop Counter-Canter Serpentine movement is from Second Level Test 1: A to C, canter right-lead serpentine, three equal loops width of arena, no change of lead; and C to A, canter left-lead serpentine, three equal loops width of arena, no change of lead. The middle loop is a 20-meter half-circle in counter-canter.

WHY COUNTER-CANTER?

Counter-canter (deliberately cantering on the "wrong" lead) is an exercise for developing the horse's straightness, balance, and symmetry, and therefore also his collection and lightness. It addresses obedience very directly. In the canter footfalls, the horse goes from the outside hind leg, to the diagonal pair, to the inside fore, so he naturally tends to rock from side to side or to canter with his haunches to the inside. Horses are not symmetrical in their ability to carry weight behind. In the trot, we can ride small circles and lateral work to target the weaker

SUSANJSTICKLE.COM

COUNTER-CANTER IN ACTION: Mary Hughes rides Revolution at the Horse Park of New Jersey in 2005. The photo shows clearly the horse's natural tendency to lean to the outside (away from the leading leg) and into the turn in counter-canter. Mary is managing Revolution's straightness and poll positioning quite nicely. The horse looks eager and comfortable with the exercise.

hind leg and require it to carry more weight. But in the canter, the inside hind leg always has the diagonal foreleg to help carry weight in phase two of the stride. The outside hind, which carries weight alone in the first beat of the stride, is the leg that needs strengthening to improve the canter. The counter-canter is the one canter exercise that enables you to target the outside hind leg because you're moving the horse's center of gravity over the loaded outside limb as you guide him around into the turn.

The purpose of counter-canter is fourfold. First, it enables you to regulate the bend that you create or that the horse creates in an attempt to evade engagement. Second, it brings the horse into balance perpendicular to the ground by directing him and his weight laterally from the inside leading leg to the outside and the outside hind leg. Third, these adjustments allow you to establish a linear influence from back to front and from front to back, thereby facilitating engaging half-halts and collection. Last, the straightness, balance, and increased collection translate to lightness and mobility of the forehand, self-carriage, freedom, and the sense that you both have "all the time in the world."

WARM-UP AND ASSESSMENT

The three-loop canter serpentine that includes a 20-meter half circle in counter-canter is a challenging exercise to do well. We often see it executed as sort of a panic event: "Can I get around and finish this part of the loop before my horse gets too strung out, loses his confidence, throws in a flying change, and everything goes to pieces?" Good counter-canter work is invaluable, but the prerequisites are myriad.

Seat check

It's important to troubleshoot and check the rider's seat and position, so in the warm-up I do some work on voltes and the strike-off to canter. If you were my student, I would check to see if you were able to keep your inside leg deep and long at the girth, with your outside calf placed a hand's width behind the position of your inside calf. I define the "seat" as everything that's covered with leather in full-seat breeches. If you're having trouble getting your horse to relax and come round in his back, your seat may be too "down" and too blocking. I'd ask you to lengthen your thigh and to distribute your weight through the entire surface area of the leather.

Leg positioning

Many riders initiate the canter strike-off by bringing their outside leg back, and then their leg returns to its neutral position at the girth. In the system I use, it's very important that riders not move the outside leg forward to the neutral position. The Second Level horse may already have been introduced to flying changes, or if he's talented he may offer them naturally. I don't want my horses to become anxious about whether or not my varying influences are asking for a change. "Marking" the lead by keeping your outside leg back in a distinct way throughout the canter gives him confidence that, until that leg moves, he's not being asked for a flying change.

Weight and muscle control

The other thing I emphasize to my students is the importance of distributing their weight correctly. You should be able to keep your inside seat bone "dominant" and your seat to the inside, not sliding to the outside of the saddle. This is a common problem in the counter-canter: The horse's movement causes the rider to slip to the outside, which results in crookedness or a flying change.

There are a couple of weight-related issues that many riders haven't really thought about. One is that the muscles of your inner thigh hold your midline over that leg. If you pull through your right inner thigh (adduction), your midline will be pulled toward the right side of the horse. This is one of the best ways to get your weight where you want it in terms of keeping it centered over or slightly to the inside of your horse's midline.

Another position problem is that many riders try to distribute their weight to the inside by leaning their upper bodies. Doing so actually puts the weight of one's lower body to the outside. Your instructor may try to help you by telling you to "push your inside seat bone down," but this directive can be confusing because muscles don't push; they pull.

To get your inside seat bone down, pull your outside seat bone up. Practice this action while sitting on a stool with your legs hip distance apart. Then, by contracting your oblique abdominal muscles, lift one seat bone off the stool. Make sure that your upper body remains in vertical balance, with your spine perpendicular to the ground. When your outside seat bone is lifted, your inside seat bone can be dominant.

Arms and hands

I often find that riders, in an effort to keep their hands still in relationship with their own bodies, are not in synch with the horse's neck, which moves in the canter. I make sure that they still flow with their arms in the working, collected, and medium canters; that the back-and-forth motion of the neck is still present; and that the half-halt works within the movement of the canter. Give the half-halt when your horse's forehand is coming off the ground to keep his weight loaded to the rear a little longer. If your hands are dead still, he is going to self inflict the half-halt in the down phase of the stride, making him stiffen or go on his forehand and more croup-high. Your hands, seat, and legs have to combine on the upswing of the forehand, while his hind leg is loaded, to increase the flexion of the joint. It is also important that you maintain tone in your hip-extensor muscles so that you do not fold or "break over" too much and lose contact with the saddle in the upswing of the canter.

Fixing a lean

One of the most common errors in riding canter and counter-canter is that the horse doesn't remain perpendicular to the ground. If your horse doesn't evade engagement by becoming crooked, popping a shoulder and bringing his haunches to the inside, he may do so by leaning like a motorcycle in a turn. If he leans into a turn in true canter, you need the influence of your inside knee and thigh to bring his withers upright. But in counter-canter, he may lean to the outside (into the turn and away from the lead). In this case, you need to use your outside thigh to keep his shoulders upright and to guide him to fill the curve of the geometric figure.

A word about bend. Riders usually develop the ability to bend the horse before they develop the ability to regulate the bend. In counter-canter, you regulate the bend to keep your horse straight through his entire body, even when he is positioned in the poll to the inside. In many exercises, you not only regulate bend and length of frame with the outside rein, but you also direct him with the outside rein through the geometry of the exercise.

It is a common misconception that one should change the bend when changing direction in the counter-canter. Your horse should remain positioned toward the leading leg, regardless of the direction of the figure. Some riders understand this but over-bend their horses to the inside in an attempt to keep them from swapping leads. This method doesn't work because, when a horse is over bent in the neck, it puts him on his outside shoulder and naturally incites the flying change, at least in the front. Even if the change is avoided, the overbent horse is crooked, out of balance, and disengaged. This approach is in direct opposition to the purpose of counter-canter work.

EXERCISES FOR THE COUNTER-CANTER

Here are some of my favorite exercises for teaching and improving the counter-canter. Counter-canter is ridden in a "counter-shoulder-fore" position. This is why I use shoulder-fore exercises as a warm-up for counter-canter work.

Warm-up exercise 1: Learning shoulder-fore

The exercise I use to teach shoulder-fore is done as a repeat exercise, not as a sustained exercise. Start by going down the long side of the arena in true-lead collected canter, and bring your horse's shoulders to the inside track. Establish the appropriate angle by heading off onto the long diagonal, and then put more emphasis on your inside seat bone toward the midline and the inside leg at the girth. Immediately establish the outside half-halt to say "Now stay here with me, with your haunches still near the wall." It's a question of showing him the way off the wall and then establishing your influence over him laterally and then longitudinally to the rear.

If your horse's shoulder comes back toward the wall after a few strides despite your efforts, don't use your regulating aids more forcefully and try to "gut it out" to prolong the exercise. That will stiffen both horse and rider. Instead, show him onto that diagonal line again. The process is a little like a wave lapping at the shore: It trickles back and then onto the shore, again and again. He may end up closer to the quarter line than the wall, but he'll learn to repeat the response and renew the angle.

This exercise starts to develop the horse's strength and his obedience to the straightening aids, and establishes the concept that you initiate the canter strides and direction more than you sustain them. Eventually the adjustments become so subtle that they are not obvious to the observer. Later, in the counter-canter, you will similarly initiate the canter and change the direction a little bit at every stride.

Warm-up exercise 2: Shoulder-fore lines

Canter on the quarter line and move your horse toward the wall with a "thigh yield" of sorts to develop the influence of the thigh aid. Next, turn onto the center line and then ride to the corner in shoulder-fore so that you're using the outside rein to guide your straight horse to the wall. (If you're on the right lead, you'll aim for the left corner.) The principle here is the same as in counter-canter, but this exercise is easier and allows you to test the influence of your position.

Counter-canter exercise 1: Along the wall

As a straightening tool, counter-canter traditionally is started against a wall of the arena so that the horse's haunches are prevented from swinging in the direction of the lead. You can use the "magnetic pull" of the wall to get his shoulders in front of his haunches and to draw him perpendicular to the ground.

This exercise clearly shows how little bend there should be in counter-canter. Only your horse's poll should be positioned in the direction of the leading leg. Later, when you're counter-cantering on a 20-meter loop, the degree of positioning will be the same.

Counter-canter exercise 2: Sighting to establish geometry

I ask students if they've ever trained in an arena that's shorter than normal and then had to adjust at a show with a standard court. They turned onto the diagonal by feel and then realized that they needed to adjust the degree of angle toward the more distant corner. In this exercise, you make that same small adjustment in each stride of the counter-canter, shifting your horse's entire front end to your new point of reference. Practice this first on a shallow counter-canter loop, and gradually build up to a 20-meter loop.

Here's how this exercise works. You draw a fan with your eyes, sighting each point over your horse's outside ear. Let's say you've come off the corner at F on the left lead and pointed your horse at E. You ride a stride; then you change your mind and move your aim over toward S. You ride a stride, assist his balance, aim over to the corner, and confirm his straightness, aim toward C, and so on. Pretty soon, you're heading back to the wall and you haven't done anything radical. This exercise is about directing the counter-canter in regulated increments so that it becomes easier for both horse and rider.

Counter-canter exercise 3: Transitions on a circle

The counter-canter needs to have enough collection that you can make a walk transition in two and a half strides. Test yourself by riding half of a 20-meter circle in true canter, then ride a simple change (a change of lead through the walk), ride the second half of the circle in counter-canter, ride another simple change, and so on.

Gradually reduce the intervals between simple changes so that you are riding them every third or quarter point of the circle. Remember that your horse's bend shouldn't change; only the position of his poll should change, by two to four inches. Otherwise, he remains the same: straight, engaged, perpendicular to the ground, and on the accurate 20-meter circle.

This exercise helps to correct riders who use too much body movement or bend when they ask for a canter lead, and it also helps to establish optimal tempo and length of stride. Most of all, it helps riders to establish a canter that is balanced and collected so that both horse and rider have poise and a sense of ample time in which to do their exercises.

Counter-canter exercise 4: *Überstreichen*

I have people use *überstreichen* (release of the inside rein) in the true canter as part of their preparation for counter-canter. Your horse should be positioned into your outside rein securely enough so that you can give that inside rein without loss of balance or poll positioning. We also practice the *überstreichen* in counter-canter work. The horse's lateral balance in the counter-canter is naturally to the outside, which educates him about the inside *überstreichen*. In a reciprocal benefit, it is remarkable how often a horse will relax and get connected longitudinally when the rider relinquishes the inside rein in counter-canter. Releasing the rein also gives the horse confidence that he won't be doing anything big, like a flying change, for a few strides. Used in this way, the *überstreichen* can be a training tool to diffuse anticipation in the counter-canter. The *überstreichen* can be incorporated into any of the previously mentioned exercises to test and improve balance, connection, and relaxation.

Counter-canter exercise 5: Partial stretch

A true test of the Second Level horse would be to have the horse chew the reins out of the hands in the true canter and then chew the reins out of the hands in the counter-canter. In a three-loop serpentine, he will naturally find the counter-canter loop more difficult than the true-canter loops. Even the obedient and technically correct horse may show a little more tension in the counter-canter than in the true canter; this is especially true if he is thinking about flying changes at all.

An excellent exercise to alleviate this problem is to ride the counter-canter portion of the serpentine in a half-stretch (allowing the horse to chew the reins out of the hands, but only halfway to his maximum stretch). To make a really smooth three-loop serpentine, it is often helpful to ride the true canter in a well-established collection and to ride the counter-canter loop with a suggestion (privately, to the horse) of chewing the reins out of the hands. The little extra release on the counter-canter loop will keep the canter elastic and forward and will eliminate the anticipation of flying changes. The true canter and counter-canter will be equally free, and the exercise will be more harmonious.

RACHEL'S TIPS AND TRICKS

Inside vs. outside:

Are you feeling directionally challenged by all this discussion of "inside" and "outside" aids? "Inside" and "outside" don't change when you change direction in the counter-canter. The inside is the side toward the leading leg, regardless of the direction in which your horse is traveling. Therefore, if you're doing a counter-canter loop on the left lead, you'll be turning right but your horse will be bent slightly left. His left side will remain the inside and his right side, the outside.

For accurate serpentine geometry:

Accuracy is as important in riding a canter serpentine as the quality of your counter-canter. Practice correct serpentine geometry in the trot. Put a piece of red tape ten meters from each corner to mark the places where you should touch and leave the wall in a three-loop serpentine. A lot of people mistakenly aim for L and I on the center line instead of two meters to the side of those points.

Counter-canter exercise 6: Guiding with the upper thigh

When you learn to use your upper leg as the guiding aid, you can become less dependent on your reins and heels. The goal is to ride a shallow slalom pattern down the quarter line, guided by your upper legs. This is an advanced concept, and it also depends in part on your conformation and on your horse's shape and sensitivity level. This is more of an experiment than an exercise.

I ask my students to ride down the quarter line and to redistribute the pressure and placement of their inside and outside thighs and knees. Notice how these variations influence your horse's bend, direction, and lateral balance. Awareness of the

RACHEL'S TIPS AND TRICKS

To keep the impulsion:

A horse will occasionally back off in the counter-canter and go up and down on the spot. The rider uses her inside leg to send the horse forward, and the horse pops a change. When that happens, I make sure that the rider can "mark" with her outside leg in a clear strike-off position and rhythm. For example, on the left lead, the outside (right) leg gives a little nudge to say at each stride, "Now strike off to the left lead. Now strike off. Now strike off. . ."

Next, I have the rider work on actually using her outside leg to encourage a longer stride in counter-canter. This is a little off-center from the standard concept of the driving leg. But if your outside straightening rein aid is correct and your inside seat bone is correct, your horse's straightness won't be so complicated at that point. You can use your outside leg to open his stride and your inside leg for a bit more jump in collection.

powerful guiding and shaping influence of your upper leg can help you to save your lower-leg influences for marking the lead and for creating impulsion in the counter-canter.

Counter-canter exercise 7: Voltes

Another useful exercise is to begin in counter-canter and then peel off into a small volte in true canter at any point that your horse isn't by the wall. This exercise can help the horse that starts to lean like a motorcycle in the counter-canter. If he begins to lean, then initiate the volte. If he responds in one beat and comes into a little shoulder-fore, you don't even have to do the volte. You use the initiating aid and then carry on, because you've now got him perpendicular to the ground in a slight shoulder-fore position, which is exactly what you want in counter-canter.

KNOW WHERE YOU'RE HEADED

The current dressage tests don't include much counter-canter after Second Level. Many people sort of survive it in Second Level and then move on. They don't use the tool and really develop it. I want to take it to a level of sophistication so that it's a preparation for pirouettes and Prix St. Georges.

That's the mind set I encourage riders to have at Second Level.

Those who have ridden at the FEI levels can bring a horse up through the levels so much more easily than riders who haven't been there. They understand the importance of the basics, but they also have an eye on the future. There may be moments in the counter-canter when you feel your horse become so balanced and cadenced that he could do a pirouette. Take notice when these moments happen. Reward your horse generously for his special efforts, and explore a little further on the days when all things seem possible. This playful exploration develops the qualities inherent in the FEI levels while your horse is not yet in a double bridle. This is how horses advance to the upper levels with happiness and harmony. They taste the qualities of collection and self-carriage in the everyday work, and they develop an appetite for them.

Third Level Lesson

Trot Half-pass

BY HANIA PRICE WITH MARGARET FREEMAN

The trot half-pass at Third Level is a lateral movement on a diagonal line with the horse bent toward the direction of travel.

BEFORE WE BEGIN

When a rider is first learning the half-pass, a common mistake is to focus too much on the bend, with the horse ending up overbent with not enough forward energy. If you were my student, before I asked you to ride half-pass for the first time, I'd have you ride several correct leg-yields (a lateral movement in which the horse is flexed away from the direction of travel). This exercise gives the feel of the forward-and-sideways motion, similar to the half-pass, and also serves as a review of how the rein aid works. Leg-yield refresher.

In the leg-yield, your horse should be straight through his body, with no bend in his midsection. His head and neck should be lined up in front of you,

A STEP TO THE RIGHT: Dr. Cesar Parra rides Furst Fabio in a lovely Third Level trot half-pass. To put the finishing touch on this wonderful picture, I'd like to see the rider's hands lowered slightly and turned thumbs-up.

SUSANJSTICKLE.COM

with just enough flexion that you can see his inside eye. In order to do this, and to maintain an even tempo as he travels forward and sideways, your hands have to "catch and release": The catch keeps him from speeding up, and the release allows him to step freely sideways and forward. If you make the mistake of holding and not releasing the inside or the outside rein, either your horse's haunches will lead (incorrect, because his shoulders must always precede his haunches in order for him to be straight through his body) or he will be "blocked" from moving sideways.

After you have a sense of the timing of the leg aids and the corresponding rein aids in the leg-yield, you may be able to transfer this dynamic to the half-pass.

I often encounter riders with misconceptions about the essential buildup to the half-pass. Some people want to ride a half-pass, but they have no idea how to ride collection. They have no idea that collection is an energetic trot with lots of push and flow. They mistake pulling for collection. With a talented horse, the collection required at Second and Third Levels isn't that difficult to achieve, and the rider may not grasp the nuts and bolts of how to really create collection. With a less-talented horse, however, the rider can't "get away with" not understanding how to create collection.

WARM-UP AND ASSESSMENT

In my lessons, I try to create a systematic flow based on the training pyramid (see page 6). The warm-up is a fact-finding mission that guides the ride. Rhythm, relaxation, and regularity (the lowest rung of the scale) must be a given in order to achieve correct contact. Contact isn't pulling. You meet the horse's mouth and hold your hands yourself, as opposed to the horse's mouth holding the weight of the reins and your hands.

As the work phase of the lesson begins, I ask my students to add impulsion through transitions within and between gaits. When the impulsion is solid, we move to the collecting phase of the work.

This can be done by starting with ten-meter circles, moving along to trot-walk- trot transitions and trot-halt-trot transitions. The collecting work is interspersed with medium trots (which often are lengthenings at first). The downward transition from medium to collection can be used to improve the overall expression of the collection. It can be hard to remember to stretch the horse down, but doing so is very rewarding within this work.

As you ride, keep in mind that collection feels powerful and that it should flow consistently. Your horse should feel as if he could push off to a medium in the trot or canter at any time. It is a natural response for a horse to want to tighten his back as the work gets more difficult. Understanding how to ride collection takes a clear idea of how it feels when your horse is right. Make a game of trying to have him always feel that way. For me, that is the daily challenge.

INTRODUCING HALF-PASS

After you've established a certain degree of collection, add shoulder-in, haunches-in (travers), and renvers (haunches-out). Then it's time to start your work on the half-pass. Here's how the half-pass aids work. Let's say you're on the left rein and you've turned left down the center line. You're therefore ready to ride half-pass left, with your horse moving sideways and forward to the left, toward the rail. In half-pass, your inside leg (your left leg, in this example) is on the girth, and your outside (right) leg is about one hand's width behind the girth. Your horse should bend around your inside leg as if it were a pillar. He should also stay in front of your inside leg so that you can ride out of the sideways-forward motion at any time onto a straight line. His shoulders must lead slightly in the movement. To help position your horse correctly in the half-pass, ride with your inside seat bone slightly more forward than your outside seat bone. This is easiest to accomplish if you think about keeping your outside shoulder and side back. Don't push your inside seat bone into the saddle; merely shift it a bit more forward. After you'd gotten the feel for the half-pass aids and positioning, I'd have you add the sideways-forward dynamic of the movement.

EXERCISES FOR THE HALF-PASS

As with any movement, timing of the aids is essential in riding a good half-pass. I try to convey the timing that the rider must feel. Once felt, the rider will often be able to produce the feel again. Many students tell me: "It feels so easy when I get the timing right."

I find it easier to start the half-pass from the center line rather than from the long side. Doing so is a comfortable pattern to the rider; plus, horses are smart and pretty soon figure out that they're going to the rail anyway. Below are some of my favorite exercises for introducing the half-pass.

Exercise 1: Circle to half-pass (illustration)

Let's say you're in collected trot on the left rein. Turn down the center line at A and make a ten-meter circle at D. Start the half-pass left as you come out of the circle, as your horse returns to D. Try to feel the dynamic of the sideways forward motion, with your inside leg on the girth and your outside leg behind the girth. You don't have to get all the way to the rail; you just need to get the feeling of how to move your horse over. Most of the time, riders are amazed at how easy it is.

Many riders have a hard time keeping the inside leg on the horse. If that happens to you, try riding haunches in on the long side and straightening your horse before the corner, then keeping the feeling of your active inside leg as you turn down the center line and develop the half-pass.

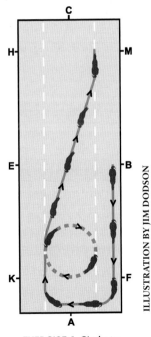

ILLUSTRATION BY JIM DODSON

EXERCISE 1:Circle to half-pass

Exercise 2: Quarter line to quarter line

I draw a diagonal line in the footing from quarter line to quarter line. Then I have the rider turn down the three-quarter line (the far quarter line), ride a ten-meter circle and, coming out of the circle, follow the diagonal line toward the near quarter line while riding in haunches-in.

Exercise 3: Changing bend from leg-yield

Sometimes a rider will try too hard and lose the ability to go sideways at all. If this happens, I reintroduce the leg-yield that we did in the early phase of the lesson. I then tell her to gently and quietly change the flexion of the leg-yield into the bend of the half-pass over three to four strides. This is a very effective exercise if you focus too much on the bend and lose the quality of the trot. Remember to change the positioning of your legs when you change the bend.

Generally, we don't school the half-pass over and over again. I try to remember to have the rider stretch his horse down. This is a great break for the horse and also a good "honesty" test because, if your horse doesn't stretch down correctly, you know that you must go back and correct the connection and collection to get him more through. Some riders benefit from taking a walk break and reviewing their work. Putting words to a feeling helps many riders to be able to replicate the feeling more precisely.

TROUBLESHOOTING

Here are some common half-pass problems and how I work with my students to fix them.

Timing difficulties

Some riders have trouble feeling the timing of the aids in the trot half-pass. If you're one of them, try to find a schoolmaster so that you can ride some half-passes in the canter. Because of the leading leg in the three-beat canter, the timing of the aids may be more clear. Although the timing of the canter half-pass aid is not the same as the timing for the trot half-pass aid (because canter is three-beat and trot, two-beat), you may be able to transfer that sense of easy timing when you try the movement in the trot again.

Overaiding

Some riders use overly strong aids in a vigorous attempt to push their horses sideways. Some horses have the habit of "falling" sideways in the movement. To correct either of these faults, begin riding a half-pass (let's say to the left) from the center line. If your horse loses the bend or starts "falling" left toward the rail, then carefully change the positioning and ride a few steps of leg-yield to the right, away from your left leg. When he is rebalanced and responsive, quietly reintroduce the left bend and half-pass back to the left. This is a good exercise because the rider has to use the inside leg both in the half-pass and the leg-yield. After you get the feeling of the correct use of your inside leg, you can use it to maintain the half-pass and to make the movement more expressive. I sometimes tell students to use the inside leg to pretend to leg-yield, but then to continue half-passing instead.

Another, simpler exercise is to go from half-pass to a straight line parallel to the rail. A variation is to ride from half-pass, to shoulder-fore with your horse positioned parallel to the long side, and back to half-pass. These exercises reinforce the horse's straightness and also the clear aids and what they should achieve.

Leaning away from the direction of flow

Falling behind the motion or to the side of the motion is a common position fault in riding half-pass. Sit toward the side of the direction in which you are traveling. Thinking of shifting your outside shoulder back is good, but I prefer to tell students to shift the outside side back, not just the shoulder. This correction helps you avoid collapsing or twisting your seat. From the ground, this correction looks quite subtle, but to the horse it's huge. It is important to sit tall and straight. Remember, "inside seat bone slightly forward" means forward, not ground heavily into the saddle.

Hands displaced to the outside

If, for example, you hold both hands off to the right while going left, the problem may be that your horse is falling on his left shoulder, making you feel as if you can't let go of the left rein. If this happens, straightening exercises are the key—such as riding straight out of the half-pass, or leg-yielding away from your inside leg.

After your horse is straight, check yourself to see if you are blocking your horse by hanging on one rein. I often will have my students push their knuckles slightly forward toward the horse's mouth. Most of the time, the horse's neck becomes longer and the quality of the gaits improves. I try to ride by this rule: When you think you have given in your hand, give just a little bit more to check.

Haunches leading

If the horse's haunches lead in the half-pass, then the exercise loses its effectiveness to create more collection. Correct this by riding shallow half-passes until you learn to lead his shoulders over. This exercise will help you to learn to feel the dosage of the aids and also how the aids work together. After you've stopped trying to override the half-pass, build back up to steeper half-passes.

Haunches trailing

When the haunches trail, the problem is a loss of collection. Remember the dynamic of the leg-yield? If you block one rein during that movement, you can't adjust the positioning of your horse's haunches. Create better connection and collection by making sure that you time your half-pass aids correctly. As you close your leg to ask for increased collection, gently move the bit a little in your horse's mouth to "catch" the extra impulsion. Don't wag his nose back and forth. All you're doing is shuffling the bit through his mouth, not pulling his head to one side and the other.

Getting out gracefully

If the half-pass develops a problem, don't simply straighten your horse onto the diagonal line because doing so encourages him to lose collection and trail his haunches. Instead, exit the movement by riding straight forward, parallel to the long side. Use both legs to ask him to move forward onto a straight line. This isn't always so easy, but it is a great correction for many problems that arise in the half-pass.

When you try this, you at first may find that your horse continues to go sideways, or that he makes a wobbly line instead of a straight line. Concentrate on getting him in front of your inside leg and moving energetically forward and straight while you remain parallel to the rail. He will learn to respond to the straightening aid, and eventually you won't have to abort the half-pass every time you feel that he is about to get crooked. This straightening aid then becomes a maintenance aid to keep the half-pass correct and to make it more expressive.

KNOW WHERE YOU'RE HEADED

After you can ride a correct trot half-pass comfortably, it's time to start working on increasing the angle and expression to develop more malleability. To help with this shift (which marks the difference between a Third Level and a Fourth Level half-pass), I often have students ride the half-pass in the warm-up at the posting trot, starting from the center line and then from the three quarter line. This seems to help both horse and rider really feel comfortable. The posting takes the intensity out of the movement and also helps to make it steeper. The horse becomes so comfortable that you can really ride big half-passes.

Fourth Level requires changing the rein in half-pass (half-passing in one direction, straightening for three or four strides, and then half-passing back in the opposite direction), and that's another part of the malleability training. This can be done at the posting trot as well. When you shift to riding the change of rein in the sitting trot, you can straighten and then change the bend in a tactful, correct, yet relatively quick way. The first half-pass must be flowing, and the transition to the other half-pass must keep flowing. This is what earns the good scores at Fourth Level. Heading into Fourth Level and Prix St. Georges, it's all about malleability, making the half-passes steeper, and not losing the flow.

Fourth Level Lesson

"Very Collected Canter"

BY CINDI ROSE WYLIE WITH MARGARET FREEMAN

"Very collected canter" (some refer to it as "ultra-collected canter") is in Fourth Level, Test 1, which carries a coefficient of 2. Here, from the USEF test, is how the movement is executed: At C, canter circle left 20 meters, with five to six strides of very collected canter over the center line.

BEFORE WE BEGIN

The highly collected canter is truly one of my favorite exercises because it is a hallmark of a well-trained horse and rider. In order to perform this movement well, the horse must be supple, relaxed, balanced, obedient, straight, and strong. All these qualities must be developed with proper work over a long period of time. The very collected canter is also an important test of the half-halt at the canter: The horse must stay light and obedient to the aids, always ready to go forward at the lightest driving aid while never running through or against the rein aid.

Your horse must have good-quality canter strides in clear collection before you start to ride the very col-

BALANCE AND LIGHTNESS: Finnegan's increased engagement behind and rider Ruth Hogan-Poulsen's very light hand are evident in this "very collected canter" moment

lected canter. He must go forward to extended canter and come back to collected canter easily, and he must be very responsive to the half-halt. For your part, you should have a very good seat and be well-balanced, erect, and supple in your posture. You should be able to apply a proper half-halt without tensing your body, pulling the rein, or squeezing tightly with any part of your leg.

WARM-UP AND ASSESSMENT

During warm-up, I watch to see that the horse and rider are both relaxed and that all the basics of the training scale (page 6) are present. I want to see that the horse is easily adjustable in frame and stride and that he can move seamlessly among the gaits and paces. I look for the rider to show that she can use her aids independently and for overall lack of tension in any of the collected work. Tension is the enemy of collection and will prevent the horse from "sitting" properly.

If you were my student, I would have you do a series of exercises before starting the highly collected canter itself, with an emphasis on transitions between gaits and between paces within gaits. Walk-canter and canter-walk transitions are especially important as preparation for this work. I would also have you ride some small voltes plus some half-pass work and counter-canter.

EXERCISES FOR THE "VERY COLLECTED CANTER"

The exercises that I'm going to give you for developing the very collected canter, as is true later when we begin schooling the piaffe, are those that truly "tune up" the horse in front of the leg but also keep him very light to the rein. Riders sometimes mistake a shortened canter that's lost its elasticity and softness for a good-quality ultra-collected canter. A shorter, quicker stride might be acceptable in the early stages of this training, but then you'd immediately add more "jump" to the canter stride again to refresh the quality of the gait. Refreshing the canter reminds the horse to maintain the quality of the strides in the highly collected canter. With the finished product, it's important that the jump returns to the canter and that the horse's forehand becomes lighter and more expressive.

Exercise 1: *Überstreichen*

Ride an *überstreichen* (release with both hands to test the horse's degree of self-carriage) in collected canter for a few strides. This is a wonderful exercise when done properly because it helps to ensure that you can maintain your horse in collection independent of the rein aids. This exercise is an eye-opening experience for those riders who think that pushing the hind legs further under the horse's body for collection means holding the front end back while driving with overly strong leg aids. They start to realize that they have to relax and sit tall and almost take their legs off rather than push harder. The rider learns that the horse will listen to just whispers of aids. The horse is thinking about going forward but is waiting eagerly for that aid to tell him to go forward. When you start to feel that you can put your leg on but your horse won't run forward through the aids, you'll feel him begin to "sit" and collect more while remaining collected under your seat. It's a real light bulb moment.

Exercise 2: Extended canter

Following some canter-halt transitions, during which I insist that the horse respond more to the seat and stay light to the rein, I then ask the rider for extended canter. This gets your horse moving forward from a light leg, measures his response to collection, and also tests your aids. The forward-driving leg aid in the upward transition should literally be just a breath. In the downward transition, lift your rib cage while sitting tall and quiet and he should return to collection easily, remaining in front of your leg and ready to go forward without resistance when asked.

Exercise 3: Haunches-in volte

This movement involves riding the horse in the travers (haunches-in) around your inner leg to start his hindquarter joints flexing. Again, you must insist on the lightest response to your aids, the goal being that he comes into a state of balance in which he is ready and willing to go forward without rushing through your aids, thanks to his increased state of engagement and collection. *Überstreichen* can also be performed during this exercise if it is done correctly. Use this exercise sparingly if your horse is on the hot side, as it can make such horses a bit tense and stiff, and also can encourage the tendency to "hop" with both hind legs.

Exercise 4: "Waiting strides"

When your horse is truly responsive to light aids, go back to riding canter-walk transitions. If he is sensitive, ride half-halts during the upward transition and the first few strides of canter after the transition, asking him to "wait" in a very collected canter for a stride or two before you go forward into the regular collected canter. If, however, he tends to be sluggish, then try asking for the "waiting strides" during the downward transition from extended canter, when the increased forward energy and activity of the extended canter will help him maintain better energy within the collection.

KNOW WHERE YOU'RE HEADED

As it's used in dressage competition, very collected canter is the predecessor to pirouette work, in which we ask the horse to not only sit and collect but also to turn. Because the very-collected-canter work has taught him to wait at the same time that he sits, he's ready for the next step: to bring his shoulders around into a proper pirouette.

The very collected canter is also a wonderful strengthening and submission exercise in general, and thus it's a link to early piaffe work because it helps the horse and rider better understand the theory and execution of highly collected work. In all of this work, the horse must "think forward" while maintaining collection from the rider's seat aids instead of being kicked and pulled together. In the introductory piaffe work, you're looking for a shortened stride that maintains the cadence and quality of the diagonal pairs of the trot. In both piaffe and highly collected canter, your goal is to produce increased flexion of your horse's hind-leg joints, with his hind legs stepping more under his center of gravity and carrying more weight behind, thereby lightening his forehand. His front end gains more freedom because his hind end actually is able to lift and carry it. We're talking carriage, not thrust, in both of these highly collected movements, but you should always be aware that this type of carriage is born out of thrust, as well.

One important note about the highly collected canter: The stride tends toward a four-beat rhythm, but not in the way that a flat canter (one lacking energy and jump) does. In the highly collected canter, because of the increased carriage of the hindquarters and the corresponding elevation of the forehand, the horse's inside hind leg begins to touch down in advance of his outside front leg in the diagonal pair that generally occurs during the second beat of the canter. This is why I've repeatedly stressed the importance of using light aids: If you brace your horse against your hand with too strong of a driving aid and too strong of a restraining (rein) aid, his inner hind leg can't step underneath his mass. He will be forced to shorten the canter stride and become flat. If the front end does not become lighter, the carrying power of the hind legs is pretty much negated.

Prix St. Georges Lesson

Canter Half-pirouette

BY MARY FLOOD WITH MARGARET FREEMAN

Canter half-pirouette is part of the FEI Prix St. Georges test and also is required at USEF Fourth Level and the FEI Young Rider level.

BEFORE WE BEGIN

Before you can work on canter pirouettes, you must have an excellent foundation in the basics (refer to the training scale, on page 6). You must have the ability to precisely control your horse's lateral (right and left) and longitudinal (back to front) balance, to give effective half-halts, to sustain his lightness, and to ride using quiet aids. Pirouettes require great impulsion, speed control, and self carriage. I would not want a student to try riding canter pirouettes until she had developed a good seat. Good "feel" and timing are musts.

Additional prerequisites: Your horse's canter strides must be of good quality, and you must have the ability to extend and collect that gait. His lateral work

SUSANJSTICKLE.COM

PSG (PRIX ST. GEORGES) PIROUETTE: Good energy and bend in this canter pirouette, as exhibited by USDF-certified instructor Christopher Hickey aboard Regent

should be solid so that you can use it to control any resistance to collection. You'll use shoulder-in to control the direction of his inside hind leg, and travers (haunches-in) to control the direction of his outside hind. He must be able to canter pretty much "on the spot" for a few strides (for more, see Fourth Level's lesson on the "very collected canter"), and to make clear canter-walk-canter and canter-halt transitions. It's also critical that he be able to execute walk pirouettes successfully. He needs to understand the position and balance required for the walk pirouette before you progress to the canter pirouette.

WARM-UP AND ASSESSMENT

If you were my student, I'd begin by watching to see that you and your horse show balance, confidence, and relaxation in all lateral work, including shoulder-in, travers, and renvers. You'd practice those exercises at all three gaits, including the walk. I'd have you do voltes to prove control and suppleness. We'd also work a little bit on shoulder-fore at both trot and canter, because that's the position you'll need to have before and after the canter pirouette.

Before I begin working on canter pirouettes with a horse and rider, I first teach pirouettes in the walk, which improve the horse's suppleness and increase his activity. He should be able to do renvers, travers, shoulder-in, and half-pass in the walk. Any time you slow something down, you help the rider to get a better concentrated feel and an idea of where the horse is at every moment, stride by stride. In the walk pirouette, you can address whether he steps to the outside or the inside, loses the rhythm, or loses the bend. The rider learns the aids, timing, and feel. You can stop the moment things go wrong. The learning happens a lot faster.

There are many variations of exercises used to develop and improve walk and canter pirouettes. Here are a few of my favorites.

Warm-up exercise 1: Box turns at the walk

Box turns, also called square voltes (angled figures with their corners a series of quarter-pirouettes) show that the rider has control and that she can keep the relaxation, connection, and roundness, all with her weight in the right place. I like to do box turns off the wall, from quarter line to quarter line in a square, because that way the rider doesn't have the wall to depend on. The turns should alternate between a quarter-pirouette and just a shallow turn, with two of each per "box." Sometimes I'll make the box a rectangle instead of a square, with longer "sides" on the quarter lines. This gives the rider a little more time to lengthen and then collect the walk before turning again. The basics of how, when, and where come into play. Too much bend makes the pirouette especially difficult in the beginning stages. If you lose the haunches a little bit, a bit of counterflexion will regain control.

Warm-up exercise 2: Transitions on a circle

Ride a 20-meter circle at the canter in both directions with several intervals of very collected canter and then medium canter. This exercise will test your horse's ability to "sit" as well as your control.

Next, on the same 20-meter circle, ultra-collect the canter each time you cross the center line, returning to collected canter in between. This exercise will improve your ability to determine when and where your horse will increase the activity, which is needed for the eventual turn of his shoulders into the canter pirouette. After this exercise is successful in both directions, try riding a very collected canter as you approach the center line; then make a quarter-turn onto the center line and halt at X. When your horse increases the activity before the turn, his shoulders can easily come around onto the center line. The halt reinforces the collection needed, reminding him to stay balanced and on your seat aids.

Warm-up exercise 3: Spirals

Spiral from a larger circle into an eight-meter volte at the canter, and then maintain that diameter on a clear two tracks. Then ride travers for two or three strides, keeping your horse's shoulders on the circle without coming in any further; then go back to straight. This exercise will really strengthen him and improve his fitness. Later, you can decrease the size of the volte and make an actual pirouette, but then return to a large circle in medium canter. Really pay attention to the position of his outside shoulder. This exercise is demanding, so be sure to give him rest breaks.

EXERCISES FOR THE CANTER HALF-PIROUETTE

When I school, I ride very few actual pirouettes because the movement puts tremendous stress on the horse's joints. Instead, I train the components. Perfecting pirouettes is more about refining the control and the balance. Good pirouettes are not possible without good balance and quality in the canter. Don't think only about making the turn, but also about being able to step out of the turn at any moment. The forward element is just as important as the sideways element. Too many riders want to do the finished product before they learn the parts. The deceptive thing about pirouettes is how many individual parts there are.

Here is the FEI definition of the canter pirouette (reprinted with permission from the 2006 FEI Rule Book, Art. 413): "The pirouette (half-pirouette) is a turn of 360 degrees (180 degrees) executed on two tracks, with a radius equal to the length of the horse and the forehand moving around the haunches... [The forefeet and outside hind foot move around the inside hind foot, which forms the pivot and should return to the same spot, or slightly in front of it, each time it leaves the ground. At whatever pace the pirouette (half-pirouette) is executed, the horse, slightly bent in the direction in which it is turning, should, remaining 'on the bit' with a light contact, turn smoothly around, maintaining the exact cadence and sequence of footfalls of that pace. The poll stays the highest point during the entire movement."]

A correct half-pirouette is preceded by a couple of strides of very collected canter, followed by a turn of 180 degrees in three or four strides, with the radius roughly the length of the horse's body. Mistakes can also be made if you fail to pay attention to the quality of canter after the pirouette: Your horse needs to maintain the collected canter when he comes out of the movement. At Prix St. Georges, the half-pirouette is performed on the diagonal between H or M and X, followed by counter-canter back through the corner and then a flying change at C.

Biomechanically, the canter footfalls in the pirouette become

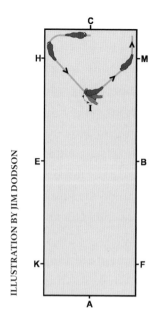

EXERCISE 2: TRIANGLE.
This pattern allows several progressive variations. After you master the quarter-turn at I, you can try a one-third pirouette at I onto the center line toward C and, later, a half-turn at I heading back toward H.

four-beat in the turn instead of the usual three, as the diagonal pair (inside hind and outside fore) doesn't touch down at the exact same moment. Because the horse's forehand is elevated during the pirouette, however, the canter appears to remain three-beat. The tempo of the canter appears to quicken as well.

Here are a few exercises that I use to develop and improve the pirouette. Caution: When your horse gets tired, you must give him a break. All of these exercises require patience and time.

Exercise 1: Square voltes

Ride the same pattern that you used in the "box turn" walk exercise above, this time making a quarter-pirouette on two sides of the square, opposite each other. If that goes well, then ride a quarter-pirouette at each corner. Maintain a slight shoulder-fore position before and after the corners.

Exercise 2: Triangle

Ride from H to I to M in left-lead collected canter, making a quarter-turn at I (see illustration above). This pattern develops accuracy and your awareness of where to go. It also helps the rider to think of the half-turn as one quarter turn at a time. You must feel the balance in each step and not rush. Repeat the exercise in the other direction, on the right lead.

Exercise 3: Diagonal turn toward the wall

Begin in your horse's easiest direction. Let's say it's his left

ILLUSTRATION BY JIM DODSON

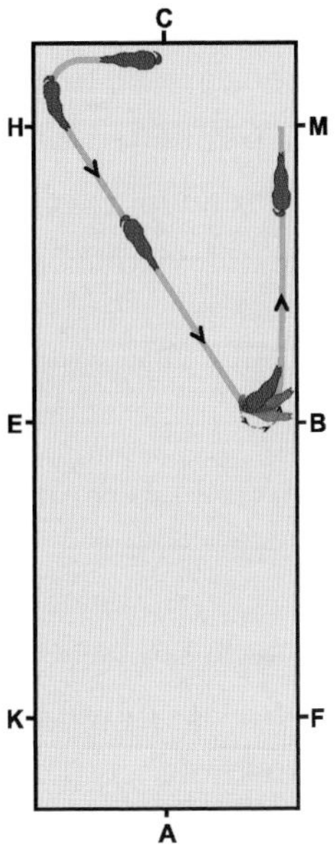

EXERCISE 3: DIAGONAL TURN. The wall acts as a barrier to help collect your horse and prepare him for the pirouette turn.

lead: Ride left-lead canter from H to B. One horse's body length from the wall, pirouette left and proceed along the track, toward M (see illustration left). Repeat the pattern on the right rein from M to E. The wall helps to collect him before the turn and helps you to feel him taking more weight behind. The turn must be performed systematically, and he must wait for you to allow his shoulders to turn.

Exercise 4: Turn from the quarter line

Ride down the quarter line in counter-canter, with your horse's leading leg toward the wall. Make a half-pirouette toward the wall (essentially a five meter half-volte at this point). Because this exercise is done toward the wall, it enables the rider to give the reins and allow the horse's shoulders to turn. The horse has to rock back, and the rider has a boundary and is less likely to pull the horse around.

Exercise 5: Over and forward

In the middle of the arena, alternate between riding three strides of pirouette and three forward strides. Then reduce to just two strides of each. This exercise is especially useful for the horse that gets "stuck" and can't get out of the pirouette because it gives the rider control of both the forward and the sideways movement.

Exercise 6: Half-pass and turn

If your horse has a tendency to lose the hindquarters in the pirouette, ride half-pass in canter, collect, and do either a quarter or a half turn. Then ride half-pass back on the diagonal line. Do the pirouette and half-pass back again. This exercise really helps to control the horse's outside hind leg. You have to be careful, however, not to use the half-pass to enter or leave the pirouette while riding an actual test, especially if your horse has a tendency to lead with the haunches too much, because you will then deviate from the diagonal line that the test requires.

TROUBLESHOOTING

Let's take a look at the most common pirouette faults and how to fix them.

Horse comes off the bit and hollows his back. Go back to the basics. Work on throughness and conditioning. Get out of the ring a couple times a week and do circles and transitions in the field to gain suppleness and forward energy. Strength is an important prerequisite before beginning pirouettes, and conditioning will really improve your horse's ability to perform this and other collected movements.

Horse turns too quickly. If he does the half-pirouette in fewer than three or four strides, he's lost his balance and probably isn't staying connected to your outside rein. He needs to wait for you. Return to the "over and forward" exercise as described on page 57. Make certain that you're sitting centered in the saddle. Riders sometimes use too strong an outside leg or sit too heavily toward the inside, either of which can cause the horse to spin through the turn because he's just being obedient. The rider doesn't realize the position flaw and then corrects the horse for something that he was actually told to do.

Pirouette takes too many strides. If your horse does the half-pirouette in more than three or four strides, he probably is leading too much with his haunches. Position him straighter and make him more forward to your leg. In the canter, alternate between the box-turn exercise and forward strides between quarter-turns, which will help to free his shoulders.

Horse swaps leads behind. This happens when the horse isn't strong enough and has lost his balance. A horse will often switch leads in the pirouette because the movement puts too much weight on his inside hind leg, and he has to relieve that. Counter-canter work will make your horse stronger, as will shoulder-fore in the canter, which also will keep him on the outside rein. Give him more time to develop strength by alternating a few steps in the very-collected-canter work with collected or medium canter.

Horse breaks from the canter. Forward and collected transitions will tune him up and make him more responsive to the leg. He needs to be a little "hot" to the leg, but not tense. However, your leg-to-hand timing may be off as well, or you could be riding with too strong a leg or too strong a hand. If your horse is very responsive to your seat aids and you stop your seat to use your leg, then he may feel your blocked hips and stop. The lightness of the aids, the calmness of the rider, and the rider's centered seat all come into play. Strive to develop an independent seat and leg so that you can combine the aids properly, using your leg to bring him up to your seat and then using your seat to direct the turn. If you push or send him around the turn, he stops and waits for you because you got behind him. As the herd leaders, we lead our horses. If you lead in your riding, you hardly ever have to send. You get a lot more cooperation.

Horse loses bend and falls in on the inside shoulder. Ride shoulder-fore to develop lateral suppleness and balance.

Horse's haunches fall in. When this happens, the pirouette gets too big. If your horse's haunches fall in, leg yield back into the outside rein until he waits. Use this exercise to teach him to step a bit forward—not sideways— with his inside hind leg.

PIROUETTES ON FOOT

Sometimes it can be helpful to ask a student to dismount and walk though the pirouette on foot (this technique can be useful in teaching other movements as well) so I can stand next to her and help her master the position and the motion of her hips. I've found that if a rider can't walk a movement, she usually can't ride it. The unmounted session can really speed the learning process. "Cantering" on foot helps you to feel the action of the gait in your hips, especially when you bend your knees and make a turn. Your legs correspond to your horse's right and left hind legs. You can get the feeling of how he drops his haunches and bends in the direction of the turn.

If a student already knows the basics of the pirouette movement, then you don't need to cover this on the ground. But doing so can be a big help to a rider with a difficult horse or to someone who just doesn't have the feel or who has attempted canter pirouettes without good basics. The unmounted work helps to clarify the mechanics of the move-

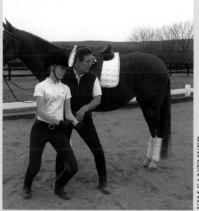

KIM SANTMYER

UNMOUNTED LEARNING: Mary Flood (right) helps young rider Kara Santmyer to get the feel of the pirouette movement while Santmyer's horse, At Liberty, looks on.

ment. I usually get an "aha" moment: "That's where my hip goes! That's where my weight goes!" The instructor can stand next to the student and position her hips and shoulders and guide her through the movement.

KNOW WHERE YOU'RE HEADED

From a half-pirouette, you can move into a three-quarters turn by changing where you exit. For a full pirouette, think about putting together two half-pirouettes. Don't think of a pirouette as a whole turn. Instead, focus on keeping the balance in each step of the turn. Make small adjustments as a preventive measure rather than waiting until the movement falls apart and you have to make a bigger correction. As with all aspects of dressage training, riding pirouettes takes very good timing, quiet harmony, good communication, and respect for the horse when he tries. At no time should you lose your patience! Go back to basics. Move slowly up the training scale. Prepare your horse properly for each new degree of difficulty. Take your time, and enjoy the journey.

Intermediate I Lesson

Canter "Zigzag"

BY COURTNEY KING-DYE WITH MARGARET FREEMAN

The canter "zigzag," is introduced in the FEI Intermediate I test. It's also required at Intermediate II and at Grand Prix. The Intermediate I-level zigzag consists of three half-passes, five meters to either side of the center line, with a flying change of leg at each change of direction. Intermediate II requires four half-passes, counting four-eight-eight-four strides between flying changes. Grand Prix requires five half-passes, counting three-six-six-six-three strides.

BEFORE WE BEGIN

Before you start work on zigzags, you need to be comfortable riding half-passes in all three gaits. You and your horse should be able to do straight and controlled flying-change sequences (tempi changes) of four strides, not just across the diagonal but also parallel to the long side of the arena. You should always be able to leg-yield at any point in either trot or canter half-pass without changing the bend and without your horse changing his vertical balance. It takes a long

SUSANJSTICKLE.COM

CH-CH-CHANGES: Sahar Hirosh and the Oldenburg stallion Coco Cavalli (by Cheen-ook) in a mid-zigzag flying change

time for a horse and rider to be really competent and comfortable executing a zigzag. This is normal and it's typical of some other difficult test requirements, such as canter pirouettes. When you learn the zigzag, as with the canter pirouette, you need to work on all the things that lead up to the actual movement, not simply drill the movement itself. If I were to tell a student to do a pirouette and just keep telling her to "do a pirouette, do a pirouette, do a pirouette," she'd end up in a tangled knot. Some instructors whose students can do half-passes and flying changes don't have them practice zigzags until it's time to do one in a test. The instructor assumes that, because the student can execute the components, she can execute a zigzag, but it doesn't work that way. You really need to have confidence and coordination, and be able to change your inside leg and get the new inside bend without panicking about it.

It's everybody's instinct to sit toward the opposite direction than they're supposed to in the half-pass. That tendency gets amplified in the zigzag. If you're riding a half-pass in just one direction, you can really concentrate and sit on that correct (inside) seat bone. You can get away with having your horse bent from your inside rein instead of around your inside leg as you should, and if you take off your inside leg, he just continues sideways. But when you're doing a zigzag, if you take off that inside leg, you've got nothing to change your bend around. Your aids have to be really close to the horse to make it smooth.

The basic zigzag is introduced at Fourth Level, in the trot. When I'm working with a horse and rider who are at this level, I start playing with the zigzag concept: half-pass left, straighten, change the bend, shoulder-in right, half-pass right. If they can do that easily, then I feel pretty comfortable introducing them to a similar sequence at the canter.

Before you attempt to ride an actual canter zigzag, make sure that you and your horse can do four-stride canter sequences (four-tempi changes) well. You need to feel that you can keep your horse straight and between your aids both during and between the flying changes. If he is relatively straight coming into the sequence changes and you ask with discreet aids, you're not changing his vertical balance. But, in a canter zigzag, you must maintain his vertical balance while changing his bend and direction of travel. Riders often get tangled up in their efforts to change so many things at once, and the vertical balance falls apart. My advice, as I'll explain further in "Putting the Zigzag Together" below, is to break the movement into several pieces and to master one piece at a time.

WARM-UP AND ASSESSMENT

When you begin working on zigzags, don't get caught up in trying to stick to the exact outline of the zigzag as it's specified in the test. The more you try to do everything at once, the more "twisted" and unclear your aids will become. The most important thing is to keep your horse as supple and ridable as possible so that he never takes over the movement in anticipation. If this happens, he may throw himself in the new direction, lose the bend, or lead too much with his shoulders or his haunches because he knows what's coming. In fact, it can be more difficult to do a zigzag on a very well-trained horse, such as a seasoned Grand Prix horse, than on a horse that's never done the movement.

I introduce the zigzag concept at the walk or the trot with my students: Half-pass to the left, bend to the right, shoulder- in right, half-pass right, bend to the left, shoulder-in left, and half-pass left. When you start to change your horse's bend, if at any moment he starts to change the sideways direction on his own, then continue leg-yielding away from that new inside leg before you ask him to half-pass in the new direction. After I'm pretty comfortable that you and your horse are getting the idea in the trot, then I'll have you try a similar exercise in the canter: Canter half-pass left, then bend right but keep going to the left. Any exercise that tests your ability to change the position of your inside leg and your horse's balance will help prepare for the zigzag. A good one to practice is the Second Level Test 4 transition from shoulder-in to renvers.

Warm-up exercise: Staying on the aids. At the trot, ride a half-pass left. Change your horse's bend to the right and continue traveling to the left, now in leg-yield positioning. Make a volte to the right and then ride half-pass to the right.

PUTTING THE ZIGZAG TOGETHER

The zigzag is always broken up into the following pieces: First half-pass, straighten, flying change, shoulder-fore, second half-pass, and so on. All of those transitions between the half-passes— straight, flying change, shoulder-fore— have to become quick and seamless. But you don't make them quick by rushing them. You make them quicker by making them more coordinated, with every movement precise, always ensuring that the horse never takes over. If you have to battle which way he's going sideways, then you're in trouble. Working outside a standard dressage

66

arena or in a field can be useful in schooling zigzags because you can just keep going. The larger space helps you to feel as if you have all the time in the world to make your changes of direction really precise. Eventually, of course, you'll have to shorten it up and make the transitions snappy. But if you have access to a really large space, you'll get in so much more practice. When it comes time to add the first flying change after the first half-pass, your horse should be straight and balanced in the change before you ever think of going sideways in the new direction: Half-pass left, bend right, keep pushing over to the left, then go straight with the inside (right) leg, flying change, and shoulder-fore. If he does that well, then you can add the second half-pass, to the right.

If your horse anticipates the half-pass to the right after the change, ride a leg-yield to the left and then go straight ahead in shoulder-in before you start the half-pass to the right. Another good exercise would be to ride a volte to the right before half-passing right. Just make sure that your inside leg (your right leg, in this example) prevents him from leaning in. Always think that, during the half-pass, you could leg-yield at any moment.

You need to completely separate the two half-passes in the zigzag movement. Never think of riding one half-pass directly into another until you and your horse are confirmed in the basic elements of the movement. Whether it takes five or fifteen strides to do that change of balance, that's how the

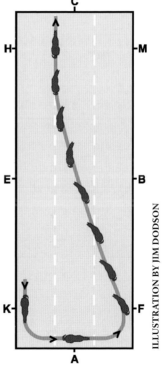

ILLUSTRATION BY JIM DODSON

WARM-UP EXERCISE: Staying on the aids. In this transition from half-pass to leg-yield, the horse's positioning and bend change but the line of travel remains the same.

zigzag needs to go.

As soon as you and your horse can make the first flying change and the second half-pass comfortably, you can add the second change and the third half-pass.

To improve the zigzag movement, practice whichever pieces you and your horse find difficult. If my horse's haunches were lagging to the right, for instance, I wouldn't think about making a flying change and doing the next half-pass until I could consistently come down the center line on the right rein and make the haunches lead. Once I could do that, then I'd do my flying change, half-pass left, flying change and half-pass right again, quickly getting the haunches to lead. If my horse didn't respond, or if he responded by going more sideways without getting his haunches in front, I would have to ask myself: Is it because my new inside leg isn't there to support him? Is the problem him or me?

When my students are first learning the zigzag, I don't pay too much attention if they're not going sufficiently sideways. It's actually easier that way for them to keep the horse's balance without throwing him from one side to the other. But before you take the zigzag into the show ring, you need to be 100 percent certain that your horse will move sideways enough when you start that first half-pass. Right before a show, I almost never school a complete zigzag. Instead, I school the half-passes, making sure they really flow sideways. Then, in the show ring, I can concentrate on the hard part of the zigzag, which is the change of balance and direction.

If you can't fit the zigzag test pattern in the standard arena, your horse isn't traveling sufficiently sideways in the half-pass. If you go five meters sideways but 20 meters ahead, that's not going to work. The problem almost always stems from the rider's inside leg not being on, plus clamping onto the inside rein. You can push your horse sideways with your outside leg, but if your inside leg isn't there you're going to have to clamp on with your inside rein to keep the bend, and then he has nowhere to go. You really have to close that inside leg, which seems counterintuitive, but you need it to form a pillar around which to move your horse. Otherwise, he'll start to tilt and won't be able to push sideways. You can't use more outside leg and expect him to go sideways if you don't have an inside leg there.

KNOW WHERE YOU'RE HEADED

The complication that arises when you have to do a certain number of strides in the zigzag, such as the four-eight-eight-four in Intermediate II, is that you actually start to change the horse's balance after only two strides in the first half-pass. You half-pass right for two strides; in the third stride, you start to straighten him and take a little left bend; you push him straight; and then you change. Mastering this complicated series requires a lot of experimenting in order to learn exactly how and where to start changing the bend and balance so that you get a straight, ground covering flying change in the balance of the new direction. Here's something to shoot for in a half-pass of eight strides: You start to change the bend in stride six, you're pushing your horse straight in stride seven, and then you get a straight flying change as the first stride in the new direction. But you and your horse might need three strides to make the change of direction smoothly, so you have to practice and feel what works best for the two of you.

In the Intermediate I zigzag, you have the freedom to prepare the flying change according to how your horse feels at that moment, in that particular half-pass. You can start to change the bend four strides early without actually changing the bend: You test your horse, and if he's a little bit stiff and not ready to change, you can stick in another stride to prepare and make the change straight.

But at Intermediate II and Grand Prix, you have to have the ability and balance to start changing the bend in the second stride of the first half-pass. You can't take another stride, and you might get stuck having to accept a bad change of direction or a loss of balance if you aren't very well-prepared. That's why it's essential that you learn exactly how much preparation your horse needs.

Another reason to know your horse is that most horses half-pass differently in each direction. He may want to lead with his haunches to the left but trail them to the right, for instance. Learn his tendencies so that you can work on them at home and compensate for them in the show ring.

Even when I work with Grand Prix level horses and riders, I almost always take the counting out of the zigzag work when we are schooling. The students tend to get so caught up in the number of strides that they start riding the striding instead of the actual movement. They lose the feeling and the precision of the horse's change of balance. The count must be in the back of your mind, but you must ride the movement by feel.

Intermediate II Lesson

One-tempi Changes

BY HEATHER BENDER WITH MARGARET FREEMAN

The one-tempi canter-change series is introduced in the FEI Intermediate II test. The one-tempi series at I-II includes eleven flying changes every stride while crossing the diagonal. Grand Prix requires fifteen changes, while the Grand Prix Special test calls for a set of nine one-tempi changes on the center line in between two pirouettes.

BEFORE WE BEGIN

Your horse should be comfortable in the sequence (tempi) changes of fours, threes, and twos before you start to develop the ones. He should have a correctly stretched, supple neck into the contact. He should be able to demonstrate the "circle of the aids": over the back, in front of your leg, and reaching into the contact. If he is short in the neck, tight in the back, or behind the leg, you must return to the basics to correct the issue or issues before you can proceed.

Other prerequisites: The canter has to have a high degree of collection in uphill balance. Your horse must be able to clearly half-halt, shorten, and lengthen

EXPRESSION: Winwood, an eleven-year-old Hanoverian shows energy and straightness in the one-tempi changes. Heather Bender, is in the irons.

71

his stride while staying in front of your leg and showing correct acceptance of the bit. Finally, you must be able to sit square and straight in the saddle with an independent seat that does not rely on the reins for balance.

WARM-UP AND ASSESSMENT

If you were my student, I'd consider several things before I'd have you work on tempi changes. First, I would look at the quality of the canter and the single flying change. I would evaluate the quality of the half-halts, your seat, your horse's relaxation and straightness, the transitions into and out of medium canter, and your ability to have him truly on the outside rein. He should be really supple so that he can be positioned toward the counter lead and back to the true lead without losing the rhythm of the steps or showing tension.

A common sight is the horse that is very tight in his back in the tempi changes. Another is the rider who throws the horse from one side to the other in the changes. I want to see that the horse really waits for the change aids and that he doesn't change immediately just because the rider changes the flexion a little bit. I watch to see that the rider can do a single change on the aids, without increasing speed and diving onto the forehand. That single change is key.

I would want to see exactly how you give the aids, both for the single change and for the sequences. Many riders grab the inside rein and drop the horse through the outside shoulder, which disrupts straightness. A rider can make a bunch of mistakes in the fours and still pull them off. You can make fewer mistakes in the threes and even fewer in the twos, but in the ones you're toast if you make a mistake. You need to be practicing the same correct aids in the single change and in the fours that you will in the ones. Warm-up exercises for one-tempi work include brief stretches of medium canter on both straight and bending lines, such as on a 20-meter circle. Bending lines in medium canter help the horse come more through his back, especially if he is more stiff on one side. If this is the case with your horse, ride with his stiff side on the outside of the bending line. This positioning will require him to carry more weight over his inner hind leg while allowing his outside hind leg to take a bigger step. Then combine the medium canter with some sequences of more collected steps on the curved line.

Before you begin work on the ones, don't focus on the count. Simply ride a couple of canter-walk-canter transitions on the quarter line, then try some counter-canter and finally a single change. If all goes well, then you're ready to try that first pair of one-one changes.

THE FIRST ONE-TEMPI CHANGES

Start by doing some sequence changes, like threes and twos on a quarter line. Doing the exercise on the quarter line instead of the diagonal will be less likely to interfere with your test in the show ring. This is exciting new stuff for the horse, and if he's showing Intermediate I while learning the ones, you could be opening Pandora's box if you are not careful.

If your horse has a big stride in the two-tempi changes, you may need to tone his expression down a bit. When you start training one-tempis, you don't want to be sitting on Mr. Flamboyant. You want to be a bit boring. He should give you a feeling of controlled energy, neither too dull nor too fresh.

Start to count (either out loud or silently) before you actually start the changes to help yourself get the appropriate tempo. Count out a two-beat rhythm, like a metronome, to help you organize the aids while you practice counting.

Walk your horse for a moment, and then pick up true-lead canter. When you think you have achieved a good balance by halting on your new outside rein, allow your new inside leg to come forward while supporting him with your new outside leg, thinking "one-one" and keeping his head and neck straight. Switch your aids with your count, making them clear yet not overpowering. Do not worry if you miss the one-one change. Quietly walk, regroup, and canter again on the true lead, and attempt to get him to change to the counter lead and back to the true lead.

If your horse goes too fast, he'll be on his forehand and will have trouble getting the one-one change. He'll also have trouble if he's too slow and not active enough behind.

If he seems to get the hang of the one-one change quickly and easily, walk and quietly reward him, relax a bit, and then canter on for a while and try another one-one. If he has trouble finding that first one-one change and then finally succeeds, make a huge fuss over him. If he continues to find it difficult, try going from counter lead to true lead and back to counter. Another useful tool is to canter on a 20-meter circle and try the change from true to counter to true again. Track both ways on the circle and experiment with a few two-tempis. Decide in which direction he finds it easier. Then go that way and try the one-one again and then reevaluate at the canter before you try another one-one. Remember to follow the training scale and also to assess your horse's individual temperament. Some take longer to get there and need bigger rewards.

Timing and balance are vital in achieving the first one-one. You can't analyze every footfall. You have to feel the horse coming off the ground at the moment you ask for the change. When I train one-tempis, I let my horses take frequent breaks in medium walk, which keeps them from getting too excited and gives them a little time out to think about what they've done.

If your horse finds the one-one change easy, then go for three one-tempis in a row and stop for the day. This work should be done in the middle of the schooling session so that the horse isn't tired. Stop with the one-one if it took a number of efforts or if he's showing signs of fatigue or stress. But a natural stopping point for a horse that finds the one-one easy is to do three ones in a row. That way, he will begin to feel as if he's really on the right track.

Just because you can do three one-tempi changes easily doesn't mean that you should try for four next time. Riders get into trouble because they get so excited when they get two or three that they start going for four or five. Stress and sloppiness creep in, the horse loses confidence, and then you won't even get one-one. Instead, your next step is to work getting three changes beginning with either lead. It's normal for one side—right-left-right or left-right-left— to be easier than the other. Instead of adding changes, make sure that you can do either sequence of threes smoothly, without feeling that one is drastically different from the other—a warning sign that you'll run into a snag when you try more than three.

It can promote straightness to school the changes on some sort of straight line with correct footing in a nice place outside the arena, where you can play a little bit. A dirt road might work well. I'm fortunate that I have a nice big galloping track around my dressage arena. In an arena, you're always going to hit the end of the ring and have to turn.

ONE-TEMPI TORMENTS: PROBLEMS AND SOLUTIONS

Problem: One change is bigger.

Solution: It is common that a horse steps farther underneath himself and with better freedom to one lead in the flying changes. Help to develop better engagement and expression on the shorter, stiffer side by riding the changes on a curved line.

I like to work on 20-meter circles, putting the shorter side to the outside of the circle. For example, if your horse takes a smaller stride when changing from left lead to right, then you'd track left on the circle, which would put him on the counter lead after the "problem" change. You may be surprised at how much this simple exercise helps the change to become bigger. Don't just keep schooling changes in a straight line; sometimes even a slight curving line can really help too. Remember to focus on the quality of change and the canter, not the quantity of changes.

Here's another solution, using the above example of the horse that is shorter on the right and that does not track as big and "under" in his right change. On the left lead, position him slightly to the left. Imagine that you are cantering with his left hind striking the ground in the middle of his two front feet (left shoulder-fore position). Keep that left positioning when you change to the right lead; then, when you switch back to the left, he may come through better. This strategy helps to develop a more even feel in the bridle. Remember to keep the same shoulder-fore positioning for both changes.

Sometimes I will try riding shoulder-fore in the other direction to see how that positioning affects the horse. It

ONE-TEMPI TORMENTS: PROBLEMS AND SOLUTIONS

helps to have good eyes on the ground, mirrors, or both to help you decide on the most effective correction.

In either case, do not swing the bend and the positioning to the left and to the right. The horse can figure out his own balance, and the change becomes bigger.

Problem: Rider gets out of position.

Solution: I'm a big believer that you don't want a lot of swing with your lower leg when you aid for a change. If you do, it causes your entire body to shift, which can make the horse's body swing from side to side in the changes. Your hips should stay pointed straight and not twist in the saddle. You've got to stay "plugged into" the saddle with your seat bones down. Your quadriceps (the muscles at the fronts of your thighs) should be pointed forward and your hamstrings pointed back, with your legs flat against the saddle. Your knees aren't open and your heels aren't into the horse. Your lower legs bend a little bit from the knee.

Too many riders roll forward onto their pubic bones and swing their outside legs too far back when riding tempi changes. These actions shift the inside hip forward and tip the rider forward in the process. Then they rotate, rotate, rotate until they lose control. Your position and aids have to stay consistent through the whole sequence and not build and build. You must stay plugged in, balanced in the saddle, and quiet and accurate with your leg aids.

ONE-TEMPI TORMENTS:
PROBLEMS AND SOLUTIONS

Problem: The timing of the aids becomes muddled.

Solution: The change aid is from the inside leg to the outside rein, so if I'm changing from the right lead to the left lead, I'm going to half-halt on the right rein, close my left leg, and have my right leg a little bit back as a boundary. If your seat isn't straight and you're giving your aid on the inside rein while dropping your outside hand and twisting your upper body to look down at your horse's inside shoulder, you may get fours but you likely won't reach the goal of twos and ones. When you change using the inside rein, you put your horse on the forehand. If you do your homework when you start riding single flying changes, it will be reflected later with success in the ones.

Problem: One-tempis are easier starting with a particular lead.

Solution: Let's say you're easily going left-right-left but struggling with right-left-right from the other direction. Riding the one-tempis on a curved line can help. If right-left-right is difficult, I'd put the change to the right on the inside of the curve. The curved line can be a single serpentine line, such as M to X to F, or a 20-meter circle. You have to experiment a little. You can also try riding a curved line from the other direction to see if it helps. Which works best will depend on where the problem is: weight-bearing, carrying, or "jumping through."

ONE-TEMPI TORMENTS: PROBLEMS AND SOLUTIONS

Problem: The horse does one-tempis whenever he feels like it.

Solution: If a rider does too many changes on a well-trained horse and she begins to lose her seat, she's inviting the horse to take over and not stay on the aids. That horse will learn to use the ones against the rider in moments of confusion, such as before the pirouettes. When the rider's on autopilot across the diagonal, the horse can come off the aids and get behind the leg.

To correct this problem, leave the tempi exercise and get your horse back in front of your leg. Ride on a circle, canter forward, or do some single changes. Be willing to leave the exercise when things start to unwind, before you dig yourself in deeper. When you're getting frustrated or when your horse is getting frustrated, walk away from it. You can come back to it later.

THE REST OF THE CHANGES

Let's say that three one-tempi changes are consistently successful. Reaching this point can take a couple of days with some horses and a couple of months with others. It all depends on their minds and aptitude. I always try to stay in the moment when training these difficult movements. I remind myself that my horse did not read this or any other article, nor does he care how long I think it should take for him to learn. I must read his mood and energy level. If he seems stressed or tired, I need to back off, perhaps not asking for any ones for a few days. Never show a horse what he can't do. Try not to make him think that he has failed. If the work seems fun and easy to him, then you can try adding a fourth one-tempi and then a fifth.

Even when I'm working on four or five one-tempis, I still do segments of one-one and one-two-three. I don't just go for five because that's the goal for the day. If I do five and I'm thrilled, I may still walk and go back to one-one and one-two-three. One-two-three is sort of the magical number for me. If you can do one-two-three in each direction, you'll eventually get the big numbers.

If things start to unravel between three and eleven changes, the problem frequently is that the rider has lost his or her seat. The horse may start to get tired or overexcited, which affects his confidence and balance. The rider has to assess what's making the changes more difficult. If you get to six or seven and then, boy, that's the end of it, something is unraveling. You may be building speed, losing the roundness of the back, or becoming crooked. You have to stop and think about it.

Say, for example, you get five changes and you're thrilled. That doesn't mean that you now add two more so that you can walk out of the ring and say, "Yeah, I got seven changes!" It isn't about the count. You always need to go back and think about the quality. I'm more impressed with someone who can do three really good changes, where the horse is straight, happy and through, than I am with someone who does seven by hanging on and ending up in a heap at the end.

When you can keep a nice steady tempo and balance for eleven changes, then fifteen isn't all that hard. You're already past the scary number at five-six-seven. But in most cases of eleven changes, you also need to think about centering them on the diagonal over X. This makes the pirouettes an issue. In the tests, the place where you start eleven one-time changes on a diagonal is often very close to where you would also start a pirouette—in the Intermediate II test, it's on the same diagonal line (FXH). Because both movements require a lot of preparation and collection to be successful, your horse can become confused and anticipate the wrong movement. I have learned from experience that the trick is the preparation in the corner, thinking about the "pirouette canter" and its positioning. For the one-tempis, I'll make the horse a little straighter with his outside shoulder when I start the first change. But for a pirouette, I position his inside hind leg between his two front feet and come down the diagonal line in a very slight shoulder-fore.

KNOW WHERE YOU'RE HEADED

Now comes the fun part. You're going to try making the most beautiful changes you can. You'll be trying to develop more expression for the rest of your horse's Grand Prix career. Beautiful changes are straight, expressive, and elastic. They show super engagement because the horse takes a big step both behind and in front—a bigger change from the hind leg and a more lifting, pointing front leg. Remember to soften your inside hand forward and allow him to reach for the change.

To me, the art of dressage is very apparent in these beautiful advanced movements. Here is your opportunity as a rider to develop through feel the best way to show off your horse's beauty and amazing athletic ability. You must experiment to see how forward you can ride while maintaining the engagement and the collection. Some horses change more expressively from more collection, while others do better from greater forward energy and pushing power.

When you work to make the tempi changes more expressive, you have to go back and reduce the count again, improving in smaller sets. One of the biggest mistakes I see in riders who are coming up the ranks is that they are too attached to the count: They're so worried about getting the eleven or fifteen changes that they're chasing the count instead of thinking about the quality. Be careful, however, when starting and stopping these smaller sets on the diagonal because your horse may "take a break" in the middle of the diagonal in the show ring. You have to know if your horse is that kind of thinker. You may want to school the one-tempis on the quarter line or somewhere other than in the dressage arena—someplace that doesn't completely relate to the changes in the show ring.

When people start schooling for the Grand Prix Special, in which two pirouettes and nine one-tempi changes occur on the center line, this opens up the possibility that the horse will start changing on his own whenever he canters down center line, such as before the first halt. To help prevent this, he must be on the aids and you must be clear and deliberate with your aids (but without a big swinging leg). If he takes over, then you need to leave the tempi exercise and ride a small circle, or perhaps walk and regroup and ride the canter forward a little bit.

I don't always school tempi changes in order: a set of fours, followed by sets of threes, twos, and then ones. I mix it up. But when you're preparing for a competition—say, for the two weeks before the show—you should get more systematic. I will practice the twos from the right lead, as they are ridden in the Intermediate II test, and the ones from the left lead. I also address the pirouette issue: One time I'll canter across the diagonal and do the pirouette, and another I'll come and do the ones. After the competition, I'll be back to mixing it up again.

Grand Prix Lesson

Piaffe-passage Transitions

BY KATHY CONNELLY WITH MARGARET FREEMAN

The transitions from passage to piaffe and from piaffe to passage in the Grand Prix test are combined for their own score, awarded separately from those for the passage and piaffe movements themselves. Example: movement 17 in the FEI Grand Prix test is passage on a loop from G to I, and movement 18 is piaffe at I for twelve to fifteen steps. Each of those movements receives its own score, and then the nineteenth score of the test is for the transitions into and out of the piaffe.

BEFORE WE BEGIN

To have successful transitions, the horse needs to have developed his own mechanical understanding of piaffe and passage. He needs to have a feel for what these movements are and how they differ.

Each horse has his own style and scope of piaffe and passage, and these individual differences need to be evaluated in the training of the transitions between the move-

CRITICAL MOMENT: Balance and rhythm are key to achieving a successful piaffe-passage transition, as shown in two frames of Steffen Peters on Floriano. His center of gravity and outline changing visibly, Floriano shows the difference between piaffe (top) and passage (above).

SUSANJSTICKLE.COM

83

ments. For instance, some horses have a very big passage, and such horses may find it easier to come from piaffe to passage than from passage to piaffe. This is because a horse with a big strided, suspended passage must learn to come under himself behind to balance for the piaffe. It's also important to consider how confident he is in his piaffe and passage work, for the success of that work will affect his confidence in his own abilities.

In all piaffe and passage work, the horse must "think forward." If he becomes at all claustrophobic or if he lacks confidence, then you need to help him to think in a forward state of mind before you can successfully attempt the work that I'm about to give you. A horse that is balanced and that wants to go forward toward the bit is a horse that will be able to do good transitions. It's not a matter of speed. The bit should be a place he wants to go to.

WARM-UP AND ASSESSMENT

If you were my student, I'd start by watching your horse and analyzing his piaffe and passage style at this particular phase in his training. Some horses, for example, naturally use their hind legs in the correct balance in piaffe and passage. Others are "out behind" themselves (with the points of their hocks behind the points of their buttocks) in both of these movements. Still others come too far underneath themselves with their hind legs, particularly in piaffe, or show an irregularity in one or both movements, such as lifting one hind leg higher than the other or taking shorter steps with one hind leg.

Irregularities in piaffe or passage usually result from one or more of the following:

- The horse does not understand the movement
- The horse is not straight during the movement (example: in piaffe, he may keep one leg behind the other)
- The horse lacks sufficient suppleness, strength, confidence, or relaxation in his back, poll, and jaw.

TIMING IS EVERYTHING

There are four parts to every movement: the preparation for the movement, the movement itself, the preparation for the departure from the movement, and the departure from the movement. That's why timing of the aids is such a key part of riding and training, and it's a part that can get overlooked.

A lot of people don't truly understand how to identify the source of a training problem. Instead of using their legs and seat carefully, or riding correct half-halts, they tend to get after the horse for having made a mistake when in fact he didn't understand the timing of what I call the "when": "When am I supposed to go from this one thing to the next thing?" "When am I supposed to go from the piaffe to the passage?" You want to make it clear to him with correct timing of your aids and half-halts.

For example, during the transition from passage to piaffe, the passage needs to collect more so that the horse can sit under, and there might be a moment of hesitation in his thought process. If, at that point, someone hits him because he didn't do it, he may become distracted from finding the rhythm for the transition. Instead, give the feeling of the proper rhythm with your seat and aids. It takes experience to really be able to figure out a horse's way of thinking. Play with the transitions, rewarding him often for his efforts.

The success of the piaffe and passage and the transitions depend on the quality of the trot work and on the horse's ability to maintain self-carriage and "sit" behind. In the warm-up, we're trying to gymnasticize the horse's gaits in general. One effective warm-up exercise is to ride trot-canter-trot transitions on a

20-meter circle in both directions. The goal is an elastic, relaxed, supple back. We want the horse to be able to articulate his joints and to relax his back, poll, and jaw.

Ride transitions within the gaits so that your horse feels that he can come forward and then also sit, remaining active while more weight is loaded onto his hind legs. Ride changes of direction through the 20-meter circle in trot, which will help him to become more equal in the reins while still maintaining the tempo and rhythm of the trot.

In the activation work for the piaffe, the passage, and the transitions, it's important that your horse feels capable of a range of collection and at ease with his balance. If he has a very big passage, he needs to be able to produce more collected, smaller passage steps so that he can come into the piaffe.

If your horse makes a mistake, especially one related to the rhythm of the piaffe or the passage, don't correct or punish him because he will relate it to the movement itself. It may be better to leave him alone and let him pick up the rhythm again himself.

Likewise, do not ask for piaffe unless you think you're actually going to get it. Prepare your horse properly in the walk or the trot before you ask. The responsibility lies with us as trainers to activate the gait sufficiently so that the horse has a chance to do a good piaffe. Never surprise him by asking him for something you haven't prepared him for, and then punish him for not being active.

TRAINING THE TRANSITIONS

There are essentially three methods of training piaffe, passage, and the transitions. One, obviously, is under saddle. Another is work in hand. The third is long-lining. All of these methods work together very nicely.

It's not necessary for a trainer or rider to know how to use all three of these methods. Many top international horses have been taught piaffe and passage under saddle only and have never had work in hand or long-lining. Still, I recommend rounding out a trainer's education by learning all of these techniques, for they provide you with more tools that you can use to help a horse when you encounter problems. Plus, they're fun! They offer a whole other relationship with the horse, and they enable you to see the way that he uses his body.

Some horses actually benefit more from learning piaffe and passage by long-lining or in hand before they do the movements under saddle. A lethargic type of horse in particular may respond to this approach because you can activate his trot, teach him collection, and train him properly, using the whip as a timing wand rather than as a weapon. You can shape his responses by teaching him sensitivity; then you can train him to do certain things easily on cue.

I generally recommend teaching piaffe first and then passage, but variations have to be made at different times during the training. For example, sometimes in piaffe a horse has to be allowed to travel (cover ground) a little bit more rather than be too much on the spot. I'd do that with a horse that sits too much under in the piaffe, to help him with his balance and rhythm. It would also help him to segue from piaffe to passage.

If your horse "climbs" too much with his front legs and gets stuck behind, try encouraging him to lower his neck during the movement. A lower neck will allow his back to come up more so he can get the feeling of having power and thrust from behind with true elevation, rather than over-elevating because he sits too long behind. With the neck lower, you can supple him a little right and left. This helps him connect his back to his neck, thus creating a comfortable place to come out of piaffe into passage. Experiment to see what works best for him.

In the beginning, until the horse is consistent and confident, I like practicing piaffe-passage transitions along the wall of the arena. I think it's more confusing and unsettling for horses to be out in the middle of the arena, where they don't have the security of the wall or the feeling of where they're supposed to be. Some horses become insecure and stop, or become frenetic and tense and run sideways because they're being asked to do more of something and they don't know what. If they're positioned on the wall, they have a better idea of the direction they're supposed to go. You can ride up the long side and then reverse and come back on the same long side. Work along the wall can prevent the horse from learning to run sideways because they "blank out" in the middle of the arena. If a horse doesn't know what to do, then he'll think up something else to do unless you're really clear and help him understand what to do. Give him an option that feels natural to him, such as traveling along the wall. On the long side, he can always go forward.

GREEN AT GRAND PRIX

Not everyone has the chance to learn to ride piaffe-passage transitions on an experienced horse, but there are a lot of opportunities to see how they're done. Many clinics, symposiums, and videos show this work very explicitly. Watch the warm-up ring at top shows. Riders who have good feel can learn to do this when they access the information around them visually.

If you have the opportunity to learn from an equine encyclopedia—a schoolmaster—he will help advance your sense of feel with other horses. If you lack access to a schoolmaster, then go to a reputable trainer who has experience with piaffe and passage. It has not always been the case, but thankfully now there are a number of highly qualified trainers in our country who can help with this work.

EXERCISES FOR THE PIAFFE-PASSAGE TRANSITIONS

Here are seven of my favorite exercises for improving the piaffe-passage transitions.

Exercise 1: Transitions within the gait

Activate the trot with transitions within the gait, including very collected trot to smaller steps and then forward again. If your horse would rather passage than piaffe, take care that he doesn't passage against the bridle instead of taking smaller, piaffe-like steps. Try practicing the piaffe from the walk if this is the case.

Exercise 2: Walk-trot transitions

Trot five steps; walk; then trot five steps again and walk again. This exercise can help develop suppleness in piaffe, passage, and the transitions.

Exercise 3: Walk half-pass to renvers

Ride half-pass in walk, ending with a few steps in renvers positioning. This exercise can help the horse understand that you want him to activate his hind end by taking smaller steps behind. It also develops his ambidexterity. Many horses will naturally begin to piaffe when they reach the wall in collected-walk renvers.

Exercise 4: Half-circle on quarter line

In collected trot, make a balanced half-circle from the quarter-marker toward the wall at H (see diagram), ending as close to the

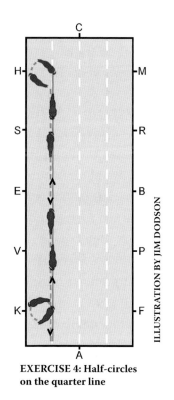

EXERCISE 4: Half-circles on the quarter line

ILLUSTRATION BY JIM DODSON

89

beginning of the half-circle as possible. In the beginning, you may need to start closer to the center line, gradually decreasing the size of the half-circle, always making sure that your horse can maintain the tempo and rhythm of the trot. After you have made a 180-degree turn, proceed down the same quarter-marker line in the opposite direction and then ride another half-circle toward the wall at K. This is a great exercise to use the wall to help your horse maintain his weight on his hind end as he stays in rhythm through the turn.

Exercise 5: Figure-eight passage

Ride a figure eight in passage, with smaller steps between the two loops and then out again in the new direction.

Exercise 6: Serpentine in small steps

In collected trot, ride a serpentine of two or three loops from A to C, simply traveling in small steps while telling your horse how good he is. Repeat the exercise in passage. Vary his neck position-ing and the length of his outline accordingly, depending on his degree of confidence in the passage and his balance.

Exercise 7: Walk to piaffe

If your horse is "electric" in the walk—really forward to the bit and elastic—you can collect and collect and collect him in the walk and teach him piaffe that way. He'll get the confidence to close his hind legs forward and to load his hind end because he's learned to step under properly.

Don't spend too much time working on piaffe and passage exercises every day. This work shouldn't be like a drill, because the more a horse is drilled, eventually the less he thinks he's good at that movement. I like to school in smaller stages. You'll be better off practicing your piaffe-passage transitions for a short time, then working on something else, then doing the transitions once more and leaving them. Most important is training your horse to think he's good at these movements, because then he'll like them. We all know this, but we get caught up and lose track of time, and all of a sudden we realize we've done too much of it.

If you regularly work your horse in the morning under saddle, it's great to come out in the afternoon and work him in hand or on the long lines for a short session—just a few minutes, and doing only a few piaffe-passage transitions. Pat him, do them again, give him treats, and put him back in his stall. When I'm working on the piaffe passage transitions, I give the horse treats only during that work. The horse starts thinking: "Wow, this is great. All I have to do is this little thing and I get treats." It's very effective in keeping his interest.

Play with the piaffe-passage transitions when you hack your horse out on trail rides. Keep it fun!

KNOW WHERE YOU'RE HEADED

Improving the quality of the piaffe-passage transitions is a matter of improving the piaffe and passage themselves. Certainly a lot of this is training, but some horses do have a gift for these movements and thus also find it easier to do the transitions.

Most horses find one transition (piaffe to passage or passage to piaffe) more difficult than the other. One transition may have more of an intermission in the balance, the timing, or the suppleness. Sometimes riders ask for too much quality or suspension in the piaffe and passage movements themselves before the horse is actually able to do the transitions comfortably. You have to feel whether your horse understands the balance that's required in each movement.

Horses that are "electric" are generally easier to train in piaffe and passage than phlegmatic horses. I call it the "dial process": You can take a phlegmatic horse and turn up his dial to more electric by teaching him timing techniques. Likewise, you can take an electric horse who's very worried and turn down the dial so he's more relaxed. It takes time to train a good piaffe, passage, and the transitions. Just don't spend too long doing them each day so that your horse maintains his confidence.

Common Threads

A Look Back

BY MARGARET FREEMAN

USDF Connection embarked on a series of lessons conducted by USDF-certified instructors and certification examiners.

The journey took us from the basic working trot at Training Level all the way to piaffe-passage transitions at Grand Prix.

Even though the topics ranged from prosaic to ultra-fancy stuff, we found that certain themes were revisited practically every month. The basic ideas remained the same, but their application varied as our virtual horse and rider became more sophisticated in their understanding and response to the aids. We would like to summarize some of these themes here.

TENSION IS THE ENEMY

In order to enjoy the journey of dressage, both horse and rider have to work without tension. This is achieved both emotionally, through proper use of the aids and varying the regimen, and physically, through stretching and conditioning.

"Tension is the enemy of collection," said Cindi Rose Wylie in discussing the preparation for collected canter at Fourth Level.

"All problems in the walk are primarily the result of a deficiency in relaxation and suppleness stemming from badly applied aids," said Gerhard Politz. "Do not limit your horse's education by working him only in a dressage arena. Give him as much variety as possible. Riding in a light seat on trails and jumping small obstacles is a good way to freshen his enthusiasm."

Mary Flood looks for ways to reduce tension when troubleshooting pirouettes at Prix St. Georges: "Work on throughness and conditioning. Get out of the ring a couple times a week and do circles and transitions in the field to gain suppleness and forward energy."

One way to reduce tension and keep both riders and horse fresh and eager is to work on the components of certain difficult movements, rather than simply repeating the movements themselves, and then to take lots of breaks. "When you learn the canter zigzag, as with the canter pirouette, you need to work on all the things that lead up to the actual movement, not simply drill the movement itself," said Courtney King.

"When I school, I ride very few actual pirouettes because the movement puts tremendous stress on the horse's joints," said Flood. "Instead, I train the components. Perfecting pirouettes is more about refining the control and the balance."

Hania Price said the same thing about learning half-passes at the trot at Third Level: "Generally we don't school the half-pass over and over again. I try to remember to have the rider stretch his horse down. This is a great break for the horse and also a good 'honesty' test because, if your horse doesn't stretch down correctly, you know that you must go back and correct the connection and collection to get him more through."

Price said that it's the natural response for a horse to want to tighten his back as the work gets more difficult: "Understanding how to ride collection takes a clear idea of how it feels when your horse is right. Make a game of trying to have him always feel that way. For me, that is the daily challenge."

Rachel Saavedra describes how the counter-canter at Second Level can raise a horse's comfort level concerning collection: "The straightness, balance, and increased collection translate to lightness and mobility of the forehand, self-carriage, freedom, and the sense that you both have 'all the time in the world.'"

SEARCHING FOR LIGHTNESS

A test of whether the horse is comfortable in collection and actually working in self-carriage, in addition to giving the horse a moment of relaxation, is überstreichen (giving of one or both reins for several strides).

"This is a wonderful exercise when done properly because it helps to ensure that you can maintain your horse in collection independent of the rein aids," said Wylie. "This exercise is an eye-opening experience for those riders who think that pushing the hind legs further under the horse's body for collection means holding the front end back while driving with overly strong leg aids."

"It is remarkable how often a horse will relax and get connected longitudinally when the rider relinquishes the inside rein in counter-canter," said Saavedra.

All of our experts returned repeatedly to the importance of rider position and the correct application of light aids. "If you brace your horse against your hand with too strong of a driving aid and too strong of a restraining (rein) aid, his inner hind leg can't step underneath his mass," said Wylie. "If the front end does not become lighter, the carrying power of the hind legs is pretty much negated."

"In all piaffe and passage work, the horse must 'think forward,'" said Kathy Connelly in discussing the piaffe-passage transitions at Grand Prix. "If he becomes at all claustrophobic or if he lacks confidence, then you need to help him to think in a forward state of mind before you can successfully attempt the work. . . . A horse that is balanced and that wants to go forward toward the bit is a horse that will be able to do good transitions. It's not a matter of speed. The bit should be a place he wants to go to."

ENJOY THE PROCESS

The two general areas that were emphasized most often by our clinicians across all the levels were:

1. Learning and training dressage is a process—a long journey that the horse and rider should enjoy together.
2. The importance of the training scale at every stage in that process.

Maryal Barnett set the tone right away in her discussion of the working trot at Training Level. As an example of how to apply the training scale, she described the way that rhythm serves a guideline when learning any new movement: "For instance, if the trot rhythm becomes irregular, that's a red flag. The quality of rhythm underpins the training scale because you'll use it as a benchmark all the way up through the levels."

The clinicians applied the training scale in some way to identify and solve problems at every point in the training process. "It's important to always keep the training scale in mind and to understand that, if you have major problems with an exercise, you might have to take a step back and find the 'hole,'" said Christine Rivlin Henke when discussing trot lengthenings at First Level.

"The reward for proper training is that both the horse and rider will enjoy the journey," said Barnett. She emphasized that improvement comes with time: "The horse should be challenged but never bored or so physically fatigued that he withdraws mentally or becomes injured from repetitive stress."

Every clinician in our series pointed out that the process of dressage training is a very individual one for both horse and rider. When those individualities are kept in mind, the process can be more fun than work, but it definitely takes perspective and a sense of the future while riding each day.

"Those who have ridden at the FEI levels can bring a horse up through the levels so much more easily than riders who haven't been there," Saavedra explained. "They understand the importance of the basics, but they also have an eye on the future. . . . Reward your horse generously for his special efforts and explore a little further on the days when all things seem possible. This playful exploration develops the qualities inherent in the FEI levels while your horse is not yet in a double bridle. This is how horses advance to the upper levels with happiness and harmony. They taste the qualities of collection and self-carriage in the everyday work, and they develop an appetite for them."

Heather Bender said nearly the same thing at the other end of the process in her discussion of one-tempi changes at Intermediate II: "I always try to stay in the moment when training these difficult movements. I remind myself that my horse did not read this or any other article, nor does he care how long I think it should take for him to learn. I must read his mood and energy level. If he seems stressed or tired, I need to back off. . . . Never show a horse what he can't do. Try not to make him think that he has failed."

That sentiment was echoed by Kathy Connelly: "This work shouldn't be like a drill, because the more a horse is drilled, eventually the less he thinks he's good at that movement. I like to school in smaller stages. . . . Most important is training your horse to think he's good at these movements, because then he'll like them."

Mary Flood applied similar principles to the training of canter pirouettes: "As with all aspects of dressage training, riding pirouettes takes very good timing, quiet harmony, good communication, and respect for the horse when he tries. At no time should you lose your patience! Go back to basics. Move slowly up the training scale. Prepare your horse properly for each new degree of difficulty. Take your time, and enjoy the journey."

Biographies

Margaret Freeman is an equestrian journalist and a USEF "S" judge from Mt. Kisco, NY.

Maryal Barnett, of Holt, MI, is an examiner and faculty member of the USDF Instructor Certification Program and an FEI "C" judge.

Christine Rivlin Henke, of Concord, CA, is a faculty member of the USDF Instructor Certification Program. She has earned the USDF bronze, silver, and gold medals.

Rachel Saavedra holds the USDF bronze, silver and gold medal, is a USDF-certified instructor through Fourth Level, and is a faculty member of the program. She is from San Ramon, CA.

Hania Price of Bend, OR, is certified through Fourth Level and also holds teaching credentials from Whitman College (WA). She trained in Switzerland with Spanish Riding School veteran Georg Wahl and his best-known pupil, Olympic gold medalist Christine Stückelberger. She also competed in Europe as a junior/young rider.

Cindi Rose Wylie of Georgetown, MA, is a certified instructor through Fourth Level, an "L" graduate, and a USDF gold medalist.

Mary Flood, a certified instructor through Fourth Level has earned the USDF bronze, silver, and gold medals. She is a past winner of the Grand Prix at Dressage at Devon (PA) and the Festival of Champions (NJ). She owns and operates Wildfire Farm in Lovettsville, VA.

Courtney King-Dye, of Sherman, CT, is a certified instructor through Fourth Level who has earned the USDF bronze, silver, and gold medals. She has trained horses at all levels through Grand Prix, and is a member of the 2008 US Olympic team.

Heather Bender, of Treasure Coast Farm in Palm City, FL, is a USDF certified instructor through Fourth Level who has earned the USDF bronze, silver, and gold medals. She is a USEF "R"-rated judge. As a teen, she was a trick rider, a barrel racer, and a jumper rider who took dressage lessons to improve her skills. Later, after turning to dressage full time, she worked in Europe with Georg Theodorescu and Sandy Pflueger-Phillips. She has trained several horses to Grand Prix and has earned numerous national awards.

Kathy Connelly, of Harvard, MA, and Wellington, FL is a USEF "S" dressage judge. She has trained and coached many horses and riders in national and international competition, including the 2003 Canadian World Cup champion and the 2005 Dressage at Devon (PA) Grand Prix champion. She is a USDF certification examiner and a member of the U.S. Equestrian Federation Dressage Committee, for which she chairs the USEF's test-writing subcommittee. She has represented the US at the Dressage World Cup, and has trained with the late Herbert Rehbein of Germany and Ernst Bachinger from the Spanish Riding School of Vienna.